All in One

This edition published in 2010

LOVE FOOD is an imprint of Parragon Books Ltd

Parragon
Queen Street House
4 Queen Street
Bath, BA1 1HE, UK

ISBN: 978-1-4454-1628-1

Printed in China

Photography by Mike Cooper
Home Economists: Sumi Glass and Lincoln Jefferson
Introduction by Linda Doeser

Notes for the reader
• This book uses metric and imperial measurements. Follow the same units of measurement throughout; do not mix imperial and metric.
• All spoon measurements are level: teaspoons are assumed to be 5 ml and tablespoons are assumed to be 15 ml.
• Unless otherwise stated, milk is assumed to be low fat and eggs are medium-size. The times given are an approximate guide only.
• Some recipes contain nuts. If you are allergic to nuts you should avoid using them and any products containing nuts. Recipes using raw or very lightly cooked eggs should be avoided by infants, the elderly, pregnant women, convalescents and anyone suffering from illness.

Front cover image: Chicken Tagine (for recipe see page 121)

CONTENTS

Introduction

Mention one-pot cooking and most people will immediately think of stews and casseroles, and these are, indeed, tasty, nutritious and popular one-pot meals. However, there's far more to one-pot cooking – from stir-fries to pilaus and risottos, from curries to pot roasts, and from meal-in-a-bowl soups to gratins and roasts. The one pot you use is just as likely to be a wok or roasting tin as it is a saucepan or casserole. The obvious advantage to one-pot cooking is that there will be far less to wash up and put away after the meal. This is no small consideration with today's busy lifestyle. As everyone tries to juggle the conflicting demands of work, family and personal life, it's hard enough to find time to cook in the first place. However, you can also save precious time before eating, as well as after, by cooking in a single pot. Once you've done the preparation, many dishes can be left to simmer gently or bake in the oven while you get on with something else. Equally, others can be cooked in a matter of minutes in a wok or frying pan. Also, lots of one-pot dishes freeze well, so if you cook double the quantity, which certainly won't take you twice the time, you can save a whole meal for another day.

When all the ingredients of a dish are cooked together, there's a uniquely delicious mingling of flavours and, just as importantly, all the goodness is retained in the cooking juices and not poured down the sink. Finally, one-pot cooking is good for the family budget and the environment as it uses less fuel.

The recipes in this book have been inspired by the traditional one-pot dishes that feature in the cuisines of almost every country in the world. Whatever the time of year and whatever your taste, you're sure to find something to please all the family. Take a culinary trip and choose from Hungarian goulash, Moroccan tagine, Spanish paella, Indian curry, Irish stew, French ragout, Italian beans, Thai prawns and much more. Very occasionally, a recipe will require a supplementary dish or pan for part of the preparation, but as a rule, only one pot is required for the main cooking. Some of the recipes include an optional accompaniment of rice, noodles or pasta, but if this seems like too much effort why not try some of the delicious no-cook accompaniment suggestions on the following pages?

Accompaniments

Even one-pot dishes can benefit from accompaniments, but no one wants to undo all their good work by using more pans and dishes. Fortunately, there are lots of easy and quick options that can turn a meal into a feast.

Salads go well with a huge range of dishes and provide a contrasting texture, as well as extra vitamins and minerals. They take very little time to prepare, but for those who are just too rushed, most supermarkets offer a range of ready-made leafy salads, mixed salads, such as coleslaw, and bottled dressings. There's no excuse for salads to be boring, as the variety of salad leaves available is vast. Add extra colour with radicchio or red lettuce, spice up a plain salad with peppery rocket, and complement the flavour of the main dish with fresh herbs. Add crunch with radishes or croutons, a hint of sharpness with spring onions or pickled beetroot, or refreshing coolness with cucumber and tomatoes.

Italians reckon that you cannot serve a meal without bread and they do have a good case with many one-pot dishes, especially soups, stews and casseroles. Most supermarkets offer an extensive range of different breads, often baked on the premises. Baguettes and Italian breads, such as ciabatta and focaccia, are great for mopping up every last drop of the cooking juices. Naan bread serves the same purpose with Indian dishes and pitta bread is the perfect partner for Greek and Middle Eastern meals. Tortilla wraps are just made for chilli con carne. Garlic bread is always popular and is easy to make or can be bought ready-made. Similarly, croutons add that extra factor to soup.

Finally, don't overlook hot accompaniments that require hardly any effort to prepare. If you've got a casserole in the oven already, why not pop some potatoes around it to bake? Instant couscous just requires moistening with hot water – do check the label before buying. Soups are delicious served with a topping of thickly sliced French bread and grated cheese, flashed under the grill. You can also add this to casseroles towards the end of the cooking time.

Essential Equipment

The most important piece of equipment for one-pot cooking is the pot itself – be it a casserole dish, frying pan, saucepan, wok or roasting tin. You will probably already have most of the other equipment you will require, such as knives, chopping boards, a slotted spoon or ladle, spatulas, a measuring jug and oven gloves.

Flameproof casserole: This multi-purpose pot can be used on the hob and in the oven. It can also be placed on the table for serving, especially if it is colourful or has an attractive design. Choose one with a heavy base to ensure even cooking. A cast-iron casserole would be your best buy, but remember that they are very heavy when full.

Saucepan: It is important to use the appropriate size for the dish otherwise the ingredients won't cook evenly, you may not have room to stir or liquid can boil over. The most useful sizes for one-pot cooking are medium and large and the ideal material is stainless steel, which can be used on any type of stove. Make sure that they have tight fitting lids.

Frying pan: Choose a round, heavy-based frying pan with a base diameter of 25 cm/10 inches. Sloping sides make it easy to slide a spatula in and out of the pan. If you prefer a non-stick finish, look for a hard-anodized lining which wears extremely well.

Wok: You can use a frying pan for stir-fries but it is much easier to cook them in a wok because the slightly conical shape lets you keep the ingredients moving constantly from the sides to the centre. A dome-shaped lid increases the versatility of a wok.

Roasting tin: Roasting tins are useful for cooking one-pot roasts. Make sure that the one you choose is large and solid, and that the sides are of an adequate height to prevent the cooking juices dripping over the rim.

Meal-in-a-Bowl Soups

Home-made soup is the ultimate comfort food and the perfect choice for a weekend lunch at any time of year. Serve it with crusty bread or rolls and, perhaps, some cheese and you'll have a filling, well-balanced meal for all the family. There are some very good quality bouillon powders and ready-made stocks available nowadays, so it need not be a chore to rustle up a brimming bowl of soup, broth or chowder.

Chunky Vegetable Soup

Put the carrots, onion, garlic, potatoes, celery, mushrooms, tomatoes and stock into a large saucepan. Stir in the bay leaf and herbs. Bring to the boil, then reduce the heat, cover and simmer for 25 minutes.

Add the sweetcorn and cabbage and return to the boil. Reduce the heat, cover and simmer for 5 minutes, or until the vegetables are tender. Remove and discard the bay leaf. Season to taste with pepper.

Ladle into warmed bowls and serve at once with crusty bread rolls.

SERVES 6

2 carrots, sliced

1 onion, diced

1 garlic clove, crushed

350 g/12 oz new potatoes, diced

2 celery sticks, sliced

115 g/4 oz closed-cup mushrooms, quartered

400 g/14 oz canned chopped tomatoes in tomato juice

600 ml/1 pint vegetable stock

1 bay leaf

1 tsp dried mixed herbs or 1 tbsp chopped fresh mixed herbs

85 g/3 oz sweetcorn kernels, frozen or canned, drained

55 g/2 oz green cabbage, shredded

freshly ground black pepper

crusty wholemeal or white bread rolls, to serve

Minestrone

Heat the oil in a large saucepan. Add the garlic, onions and Parma ham and cook over a medium heat, stirring, for 3 minutes, until slightly softened. Add the red and orange peppers and the chopped tomatoes and cook for a further 2 minutes, stirring. Stir in the stock, then add the celery. Drain and add the borlotti beans along with the cabbage, peas and parsley. Season with salt and pepper. Bring to the boil, then lower the heat and simmer for 30 minutes.

Add the vermicelli to the pan. Cook for a further 10–12 minutes, or according to the instructions on the packet. Remove from the heat and ladle into serving bowls. Garnish with freshly grated Parmesan and serve with fresh crusty bread.

SERVES 4

2 tbsp olive oil

2 garlic cloves, chopped

2 red onions, chopped

75 g/2^3/$_4$ oz Parma ham, sliced

1 red pepper, deseeded and chopped

1 orange pepper, deseeded and chopped

400 g/14 oz canned chopped tomatoes

1 litre/1^3/$_4$ pints vegetable stock

1 celery stick, trimmed and sliced

400 g/14 oz canned borlotti beans

100 g/3^1/$_2$ oz green leafy cabbage, shredded

75 g/2^3/$_4$ oz frozen peas, defrosted

1 tbsp chopped fresh parsley

salt and pepper

75 g/2^3/$_4$ oz dried vermicelli

freshly grated Parmesan cheese, to garnish

fresh crusty bread, to serve

French Onion Soup

Thinly slice the onions. Heat the olive oil in a large, heavy-based saucepan, then add the onions and cook, stirring occasionally, for 10 minutes, until they are just beginning to brown. Stir in the chopped garlic, sugar and thyme, then reduce the heat and cook, stirring occasionally, for 30 minutes, or until the onions are golden brown.

Sprinkle in the flour and cook, stirring for 1–2 minutes. Stir in the wine. Gradually stir in the stock and bring to the boil, skimming off any scum that rises to the surface, then reduce the heat and simmer for 45 minutes. Meanwhile, preheat the grill to medium. Toast the bread on both sides under the grill. Rub the toast with the garlic clove.

Ladle the soup into 6 flameproof bowls set on a baking sheet. Float a piece of toast in each bowl and divide the grated cheese among them. Place under the preheated grill for 2–3 minutes, or until the cheese has just melted. Garnish with thyme and serve.

SERVES 6

675 g/1 lb 8 oz onions

3 tbsp olive oil

4 garlic cloves, 3 chopped and 1 peeled but kept whole

1 tsp sugar

2 tsp chopped fresh thyme

2 tbsp plain flour

125 ml/4 fl oz dry white wine

2 litres/3½ pints vegetable stock

6 slices of French bread

300 g/10½ oz Gruyère cheese, grated

fresh thyme sprigs, to garnish

Borscht

Slice the onion into rings. Melt the butter in a large, heavy-based saucepan. Add the onion and cook over a low heat, stirring occasionally, for 3–5 minutes, or until softened. Add the beetroot batons, carrot, celery and chopped tomatoes and cook, stirring frequently, for 4–5 minutes.

Add the stock, vinegar, sugar and 1 tablespoon of the snipped dill into the saucepan. Season to taste with salt and pepper. Bring to the boil, reduce the heat and simmer for 35–40 minutes, or until the vegetables are tender.

Stir in the cabbage, cover and simmer for 10 minutes. Stir in the grated beetroot, with any juices, and cook for a further 10 minutes. Ladle into warmed bowls. Garnish with a spoonful of soured cream and the other tablespoon of snipped dill and serve with crusty bread.

SERVES 6

1 onion

55 g/2 oz butter

350 g/12 oz raw beetroot,
   cut into thin batons, and
   1 raw beetroot, grated

1 carrot, cut into thin batons

3 celery sticks, thinly sliced

2 tomatoes, peeled,
   deseeded and chopped

1.4 litres/$2^1/_2$ pints vegetable stock

1 tbsp white wine vinegar

1 tbsp sugar

2 tbsp snipped fresh dill

salt and pepper

115 g/4 oz white cabbage, shredded

150 ml/5 fl oz soured cream,
   to garnish

crusty bread, to serve (optional)

Mexican-style Beef & Rice Soup

Heat half the oil in a large saucepan over a medium–high heat. Add the meat in one layer and cook until well browned, turning to colour all sides. Using a slotted spoon, transfer the meat to a plate. Drain off the oil and wipe out the pan with kitchen paper.

Heat the remaining oil in the saucepan over a medium heat. Add the onion, cover and cook for about 3 minutes, stirring occasionally, until just softened. Add the green pepper, chilli, garlic and carrot, and continue cooking, covered, for 3 minutes.

Add the coriander, cumin, cinnamon, oregano, bay leaf and orange rind. Stir in the tomatoes and stock, along with the beef and wine. Bring almost to the boil and when the mixture begins to bubble, reduce the heat to low. Cover and simmer gently, stirring occasionally, for about 1 hour until the meat is tender.

Stir in the rice, raisins and chocolate, and continue cooking, stirring occasionally, for about 30 minutes until the rice is tender.

Ladle into warmed bowls and garnish with coriander.

SERVES 4

3 tbsp olive oil

500 g/1 lb 2 oz boneless stewing beef, cut into 2.5-cm/1-inch pieces

1 onion, finely chopped

1 green pepper, cored, deseeded and finely chopped

1 small fresh red chilli, deseeded and finely chopped

2 garlic cloves, finely chopped

1 carrot, finely chopped

$^1/_4$ tsp ground coriander

$^1/_4$ tsp ground cumin

$^1/_8$ tsp ground cinnamon

$^1/_4$ tsp dried oregano

1 bay leaf

grated rind of $^1/_2$ orange

400 g/14 oz canned chopped tomatoes

1.2 litres/2 pints beef stock

150 ml/5 fl oz red wine

50 g/1$^3/_4$ oz long-grain white rice

25 g/1 oz/3 tbsp raisins

15 g/$^1/_2$ oz plain chocolate, melted

chopped fresh coriander, to garnish

Spicy Lamb Soup with Chickpeas & Courgettes

Heat the oil in a large saucepan or cast-iron casserole over a medium–high heat. Add the lamb, in batches if necessary to avoid crowding the pan, and cook until evenly browned on all sides, adding a little more oil if needed. Remove the meat with a slotted spoon when browned.

Reduce the heat and add the onion and garlic to the pan. Cook, stirring frequently, for 1–2 minutes.

Add the water and return all the meat to the pan. Bring just to the boil and skim off any scum that rises to the surface. Reduce the heat and stir in the tomatoes, bay leaf, thyme, oregano, cinnamon, cumin, turmeric and harissa. Simmer for about 1 hour, or until the meat is very tender. Discard the bay leaf.

Stir in the chickpeas, carrot and potato and simmer for 15 minutes. Add the courgette and peas and continue simmering for 15–20 minutes, or until all the vegetables are tender.

Adjust the seasoning, adding more harissa, if desired. Ladle the soup into warmed bowls and garnish with mint or coriander.

SERVES 4–6

1–2 tbsp olive oil

450 g/1 lb lean boneless lamb, such as shoulder or neck fillet, trimmed of fat and cut into 1-cm/$1/2$-inch cubes

1 onion, finely chopped

2–3 garlic cloves, crushed

1.2 litres/2 pints water

400 g/14 oz canned chopped tomatoes in juice

1 bay leaf

$1/2$ tsp dried thyme

$1/2$ tsp dried oregano

$1/8$ tsp ground cinnamon

$1/4$ tsp ground cumin

$1/4$ tsp ground turmeric

1 tsp harissa, or more to taste

400 g/14 oz canned chickpeas, rinsed and drained

1 carrot, diced

1 potato, diced

1 courgette, quartered lengthways and sliced

100 g/$31/2$ oz fresh or defrosted frozen green peas

sprigs of fresh mint or coriander, to garnish

Scotch Broth

Cut the meat into small pieces, removing as much fat as possible. Put into a large saucepan and cover with the water. Bring to the boil over a medium heat and skim off any scum that appears.

Add the pearl barley, reduce the heat and cook gently, covered, for 1 hour.

Add the prepared vegetables and season well with salt and pepper. Continue to cook for a further hour. Remove from the heat and allow to cool slightly.

Remove the meat from the saucepan using a slotted spoon and strip the meat from the bones. Discard the bones and any fat or gristle. Place the meat back in the saucepan and leave to cool thoroughly, then refrigerate overnight.

Scrape the solidified fat off the surface of the soup. Reheat, season with salt and pepper to taste and serve piping hot, garnished with the parsley scattered over the top.

SERVES 6–8

700 g/1 lb 9 oz neck of lamb

1.7 litres/3 pints water

55 g/2 oz pearl barley

2 onions, chopped

1 garlic clove, finely chopped

3 small turnips, diced

3 carrots, peeled and thinly sliced

2 celery sticks, sliced

2 leeks, sliced

salt and pepper

2 tbsp chopped fresh parsley,
  to garnish

Pork Chilli Soup

Heat the oil in a large saucepan over a medium–high heat. Add the pork, season with salt and pepper, and cook until no longer pink, stirring frequently. Reduce the heat to medium and add the onion, celery, pepper and garlic. Cover and continue cooking for 5 minutes, stirring occasionally, until the onion is softened.

Add the tomatoes, tomato purée and stock. Add the coriander, cumin, oregano and chilli powder. Stir the ingredients in to combine well.

Bring just to the boil, reduce the heat to low, cover and simmer for 30–40 minutes until all the vegetables are very tender. Taste and adjust the seasoning, adding more chilli powder if you like it hotter.

Ladle the chilli into warmed bowls and sprinkle with coriander or parsley. Pass the soured cream separately, or top each serving with a spoonful.

SERVES 4

2 tsp olive oil

500 g/1 lb 2 oz lean minced pork

salt and pepper

1 onion, finely chopped

1 celery stick, finely chopped

1 red or green pepper, cored, deseeded and finely chopped

2–3 garlic cloves, finely chopped

400 g/14 oz canned chopped tomatoes in juice

3 tbsp tomato purée

450 ml/16 fl oz chicken or meat stock

$1/8$ tsp ground coriander

$1/8$ tsp ground cumin

$1/4$ tsp dried oregano

1 tsp mild chilli powder, or to taste

chopped fresh coriander leaves or parsley, to garnish

soured cream, to serve

Bacon & Lentil Soup

Heat a large, heavy-based saucepan or flameproof casserole. Add the bacon and cook over a medium heat, stirring, for 4–5 minutes, or until the fat runs. Add the chopped onion, carrots, celery, turnip and potato and cook, stirring frequently, for 5 minutes.

Add the lentils and bouquet garni and pour in the water or stock. Bring to the boil, reduce the heat and simmer for 1 hour, or until the lentils are tender.

Remove and discard the bouquet garni and season the soup to taste with pepper, and with salt, if necessary. Ladle into warmed soup bowls and serve immediately.

SERVES 4

450 g/1 lb thick, rindless smoked bacon rashers, diced

1 onion, chopped

2 carrots, sliced

2 celery sticks, chopped

1 turnip, chopped

1 large potato, chopped

85 g/3 oz Puy lentils

1 bouquet garni

1 litre/1^{3}/$_{4}$ pints water or chicken stock

salt and pepper

Chorizo & Red Kidney Bean Soup

Heat the oil in a large saucepan. Add the garlic and onions and cook over a medium heat, stirring, for 3 minutes, until slightly softened. Add the red pepper and cook for a further 3 minutes, stirring. In a bowl, mix the cornflour with enough stock to make a smooth paste and stir it into the pan. Cook, stirring, for 2 minutes. Stir in the remaining stock, then add the potatoes and season with salt and pepper. Bring to the boil, then lower the heat and simmer for 25 minutes, until the vegetables are tender.

Add the chorizo, courgettes and kidney beans to the pan. Cook for 10 minutes, then stir in the cream and cook for a further 5 minutes. Remove from the heat and ladle into serving bowls. Serve with slices of fresh bread.

SERVES 4

2 tbsp olive oil

2 garlic cloves, chopped

2 red onions, chopped

1 red pepper, deseeded and chopped

2 tbsp cornflour

1 litre/1³/₄ pints vegetable stock

450 g/1 lb potatoes, peeled, halved and sliced

salt and pepper

150 g/5¹/₂ oz chorizo, sliced

2 courgettes, trimmed and sliced

200 g/7 oz canned red kidney beans, drained

125 ml/4 fl oz double cream

thick slices of fresh bread, to serve

Cock-a-leekie Soup

Heat the oil in a large saucepan over a medium heat, then add the onions, carrots and 2 roughly chopped leeks. Sauté for 3–4 minutes until just golden brown.

Wipe the chicken inside and out and remove any excess skin and fat.

Place the chicken in the saucepan with the cooked vegetables and add the bay leaves. Pour in enough cold water to just cover and season well with salt and pepper. Bring to the boil, reduce the heat, then cover and simmer for 1–1^1/2 hours. From time to time skim off any scum that forms.

Remove the chicken from the stock, skin, then remove all the meat. Cut the meat into neat pieces.

Strain the stock through a colander, discard the vegetables and bay leaves and return to the rinsed-out saucepan. Expect to have 1.2–1.4 litres/2–2^1/2 pints of stock. If you have time, it is a good idea to allow the stock to cool so that the fat may be removed. If not, blot the fat off the surface with pieces of kitchen paper.

Heat the stock to the simmering point, add the sliced leeks and prunes to the saucepan and heat for about 1 minute.

Return the chicken to the pan and heat through. Serve immediately in warmed deep dishes. Garnish with the parsley.

SERVES 6–8

2 tbsp vegetable or olive oil

2 onions, roughly chopped

2 carrots, roughly chopped

5 leeks, 2 roughly chopped,
   3 thinly sliced

1 chicken, weighing 1.3 kg/3 lb

2 bay leaves

salt and pepper

6 prunes, sliced

sprigs of fresh parsley, to garnish

Chicken-Noodle Soup

Put the chicken breasts and water in a saucepan over a high heat and bring to the boil. Lower the heat to its lowest setting and simmer, skimming the surface until no more foam rises. Add the onion, garlic, ginger, peppercorns, cloves, star anise and a pinch of salt, and continue to simmer for 20 minutes, or until the chicken is tender and cooked through. Meanwhile, grate the carrot along its length on the coarse side of a grater so you get long, thin strips.

Strain the chicken, reserving about 1.2 litres/2 pints stock, but discarding any flavouring solids. (At this point you can leave the stock to cool and refrigerate overnight, so any fat solidifies and can be lifted off and discarded.) Return the stock to the rinsed-out saucepan with the carrot, celery, baby sweetcorn and spring onions and bring to the boil. Boil until the baby sweetcorn are almost tender, then add the noodles and continue boiling for 2 minutes.

Meanwhile, chop the chicken, add to the pan and continue cooking for about 1 minute longer until the chicken is reheated and the noodles are soft. Add seasoning to taste.

SERVES 4–6

2 skinless chicken breasts

2 litres/$3^{1}/_{2}$ pints water

1 onion, unpeeled, cut in half

1 large garlic clove, cut in half

1-cm/$^{1}/_{2}$-inch piece fresh root
    ginger, peeled and sliced

4 black peppercorns, lightly crushed

4 cloves

2 star anise

salt and pepper

1 carrot, peeled

1 celery stick, chopped

100 g/$3^{1}/_{2}$ oz baby sweetcorn, cut
    in half lengthways and chopped

2 spring onions, finely shredded

115 g/4 oz dried rice vermicelli
    noodles

Turkey & Lentil Soup

Heat the oil in a large saucepan. Add the garlic and onion and cook over a medium heat, stirring, for 3 minutes, until slightly softened. Add the mushrooms, red pepper and tomatoes and cook for a further 5 minutes, stirring. Pour in the stock and red wine, then add the cauliflower, carrot and red lentils. Season with salt and pepper. Bring to the boil, then lower the heat and simmer the soup gently for 25 minutes, until the vegetables are tender and cooked through.

Add the turkey and courgette to the pan and cook for 10 minutes. Stir in the shredded basil and cook for a further 5 minutes, then remove from the heat and ladle into serving bowls. Garnish with basil leaves and serve with fresh crusty bread.

SERVES 4

1 tbsp olive oil

1 garlic clove, chopped

1 large onion, chopped

200 g/7 oz mushrooms, sliced

1 red pepper, deseeded and
  chopped

6 tomatoes, skinned, deseeded
  and chopped

1.2 litre/2 pints chicken stock

150 ml/5 fl oz red wine

85 g/3 oz cauliflower florets

1 carrot, peeled and chopped

200 g/7 oz red lentils

salt and pepper

350 g/12 oz cooked turkey meat,
  chopped

1 courgette, trimmed and chopped

1 tbsp shredded fresh basil

basil leaves, to garnish

thick slices of fresh crusty bread,
  to serve

Clam & Corn Chowder

Melt the butter in a large saucepan over a low–medium heat. Add the onion and carrot and cook for 3–4 minutes, stirring frequently, until the onion is softened. Stir in the flour and continue cooking for 2 minutes.

Slowly add about half the stock and stir well, scraping the bottom of the pan to mix in the flour. Pour in the remaining stock and the water and bring just to the boil, stirring.

Add the potatoes, sweetcorn and milk and stir to combine. Reduce the heat and simmer gently, partially covered, for about 20 minutes, stirring occasionally, until all the vegetables are tender.

Chop the clams, if large. Stir in the clams and continue cooking for about 5 minutes until heated through. Taste and adjust the seasoning, if needed.

Ladle the soup into bowls and sprinkle with parsley.

SERVES 4

4 tsp butter

1 large onion, finely chopped

1 small carrot, finely diced

3 tbsp plain flour

300 ml/10 fl oz fish stock

200 ml/7 fl oz water

450 g/1 lb potatoes, diced

125 g/4 oz cooked or defrosted frozen sweetcorn

450 ml/16 fl oz full-fat milk

280 g/10 oz canned clams, drained and rinsed

salt and pepper

chopped fresh parsley, to garnish

Laksa

Heat the oil in a large saucepan over a medium heat, add the garlic, chillies, lemon grass and ginger and cook for 5 minutes, stirring frequently. Add the stock and bring to the boil, then reduce the heat and simmer for 5 minutes.

Stir in the prawns, mushrooms and carrot. If using the egg noodles, break into small lengths, add to the saucepan and simmer for a further 5 minutes, or until the prawns have turned pink and the noodles are tender.

Stir in the Thai fish sauce and coriander and heat through for a further minute before serving.

SERVES 4

1 tbsp sunflower oil

2–3 garlic cloves, cut into thin slivers

1–2 fresh red Thai chillies, deseeded and sliced

2 lemon grass stalks, outer leaves removed, chopped

2.5-cm / 1-inch piece fresh root ginger, grated

1.2 litres / 2 pints fish or vegetable stock

350 g / 12 oz large raw prawns, peeled and deveined

115 g / 4 oz shiitake mushrooms, sliced

1 large carrot, grated

55 g / 2 oz dried egg noodles (optional)

1–2 tsp Thai fish sauce

1 tbsp chopped fresh coriander

Bouillabaisse

Soak the mussels in lightly salted water for 10 minutes. Scrub the shells under cold running water and pull off any beards. Discard any with broken shells. Tap the remaining mussels and discard any that refuse to close. Put the rest into a large pan with a little water, bring to the boil and cook over high heat for 4 minutes. Transfer the cooked mussels to a bowl, discarding any that remain closed, and reserve. Wipe out the pan with kitchen paper.

Heat the oil in the pan over a medium heat. Add the garlic and onions and cook, stirring, for 3 minutes. Stir in the tomatoes, stock, wine, bay leaf, saffron and herbs. Bring to the boil, reduce the heat, cover and simmer for 30 minutes.

When the tomato mixture is cooked, rinse the fish fillets, pat dry and cut into chunks. Add to the pan and simmer for 5 minutes. Add the mussels, prawns and scallops and season with salt and pepper. Cook for 3 minutes, until the fish is cooked through.

Remove from the heat, discard the bay leaf and ladle into serving bowls. Serve with fresh baguettes.

SERVES 4

200 g/7 oz live mussels

100 ml/$3^{1}/_{2}$ fl oz olive oil

3 garlic cloves, chopped

2 onions, chopped

2 tomatoes, deseeded and chopped

700 ml/$1^{1}/_{4}$ pints fish stock

400 ml/14 fl oz white wine

1 bay leaf

pinch of saffron threads

2 tbsp chopped fresh basil

2 tbsp chopped fresh parsley

250 g/9 oz snapper or monkfish fillets

250 g/9 oz haddock fillets, skinned

200 g/7 oz prawns, peeled and deveined

100 g/$3^{1}/_{2}$ oz scallops

salt and pepper

fresh baguettes, to serve

Meat Feasts

This chapter features slow-cooked, succulent stews and casseroles that simply melt deliciously in the mouth, whether beef, lamb or pork. They have the additional benefit of being extremely economical because they use the less expensive cuts of meat. However, quicker-cooked but just as tasty dishes, such as a Chinese-style stir-fry and a Tex-Mex chilli, are also included and it would, of course, have been simply criminal to omit classic pot roasts.

Pot Roast with Potatoes & Dill

Preheat the oven to 140°C/275°F/Gas Mark 1. Mix 2 tablespoons of the flour with the salt and pepper in a shallow dish. Dip the meat to coat. Heat the oil in a flameproof casserole and brown the meat all over. Transfer to a plate. Add half the butter to the casserole and cook the onion, celery, carrots, dill seed and thyme for 5 minutes. Return the meat and juices to the casserole.

Pour in the wine and enough stock to reach one-third of the way up the meat. Bring to the boil, cover and cook in the oven for 3 hours, turning the meat every 30 minutes. After it has been cooking for 2 hours, add the potatoes and more stock if necessary.

When ready, transfer the meat and vegetables to a warmed serving dish. Strain the cooking liquid to remove any solids, then return the liquid to the casserole.

Mix the remaining butter and flour to a paste. Bring the cooking liquid to the boil. Whisk in small pieces of the flour and butter paste, whisking constantly until the sauce is smooth. Pour the sauce over the meat and vegetables. Sprinkle with the fresh dill to serve.

SERVES 6

$2^1/_2$ tbsp plain flour

1 tsp salt

$^1/_4$ tsp pepper

1 rolled brisket joint, weighing 1.6 kg/3 lb 8 oz

2 tbsp vegetable oil

2 tbsp butter

1 onion, finely chopped

2 celery sticks, diced

2 carrots, peeled and diced

1 tsp dill seed

1 tsp dried thyme or oregano

350 ml/12 fl oz red wine

150–225 ml/5–8 fl oz beef stock

4–5 potatoes, cut into large chunks and boiled until just tender

2 tbsp chopped fresh dill, to serve

Beef in Beer with Herb Dumplings

Preheat the oven to 160°C/325°F/Gas Mark 3. Heat the oil in a flameproof casserole. Add the onions and carrots and cook over a low heat, stirring occasionally, for 5 minutes, or until the onions are softened. Meanwhile, place the flour in a polythene bag and season with salt and pepper. Add the stewing steak to the bag, tie the top and shake well to coat. Do this in batches, if necessary.

Remove the vegetables from the casserole with a slotted spoon and reserve. Add the stewing steak to the casserole, in batches, and cook, stirring frequently, until browned all over. Return all the meat and the onions and carrots to the casserole and sprinkle in any remaining seasoned flour. Pour in the stout and add the sugar, bay leaves and thyme. Bring to the boil, cover and transfer to the preheated oven to bake for 1¾ hours.

To make the herb dumplings, sift the flour and salt into a bowl. Stir in the suet and parsley and add enough of the water to make a soft dough. Shape into small balls between the palms of your hands. Add to the casserole and return to the oven for 30 minutes. Remove and discard the bay leaves. Serve immediately, sprinkled with chopped parsley.

SERVES 6

2 tbsp sunflower oil

2 large onions, thinly sliced

8 carrots, sliced

4 tbsp plain flour

salt and pepper

1.25 kg/2 lb 12 oz stewing steak, cut into cubes

425 ml/15 fl oz stout

2 tsp muscovado sugar

2 bay leaves

1 tbsp chopped fresh thyme

for the herb dumplings

115 g/4 oz self-raising flour

pinch of salt

55 g/2 oz shredded suet

2 tbsp chopped fresh parsley, plus extra to garnish

about 4 tbsp water

Daube of Beef

Combine the wine, brandy, vinegar, shallots, carrots, garlic, peppercorns, thyme, rosemary, parsley and bay leaf, and season to taste with salt. Add the beef, stirring to coat, then cover with clingfilm and leave in the refrigerator to marinate for 8 hours, or overnight.

Preheat the oven to 150°C/300°F/Gas Mark 2. Drain the beef, reserving the marinade, and pat dry on kitchen paper. Heat half the oil in a large, flameproof casserole. Add the beef in batches and cook over a medium heat, stirring, for 3–4 minutes, or until browned. Transfer the beef to a plate with a slotted spoon. Brown the remaining beef, adding more oil, if necessary.

Return all of the beef to the casserole and add the tomatoes and their juices, mushrooms and orange rind. Sieve the reserved marinade into the casserole. Bring to the boil, cover and cook in the oven for 2½ hours.

Remove the casserole from the oven, add the ham and olives and return it to the oven to cook for a further 30 minutes, or until the beef is very tender. Discard the orange rind and serve straight from the casserole, garnished with parsley.

SERVES 6

350 ml/12 fl oz dry white wine

2 tbsp brandy

1 tbsp white wine vinegar

4 shallots, sliced

4 carrots, sliced

1 garlic clove, finely chopped

6 black peppercorns

4 fresh thyme sprigs

1 fresh rosemary sprig

2 fresh parsley sprigs, plus extra
   to garnish

1 bay leaf

salt

750 g/1 lb 10 oz beef topside, cut
   into 2.5-cm/1-inch cubes

2 tbsp olive oil

800 g/1 lb 12 oz canned chopped
   tomatoes

225 g/8 oz mushrooms, sliced

strip of finely pared orange rind

55 g/2 oz Bayonne ham, cut
   into strips

12 black olives

Beef Goulash

Heat the vegetable oil in a large frying pan and cook the onion and garlic for 3–4 minutes.

Cut the stewing steak into chunks and cook over a high heat for 3 minutes until browned all over. Add the paprika and stir well, then add the chopped tomatoes, tomato purée, pepper and mushrooms. Cook for 2 minutes, stirring frequently.

Pour in the beef stock. Bring to the boil, then reduce the heat. Cover and simmer for 1½–2 hours until the meat is tender.

Blend the cornflour with the water, then add to the pan, stirring until thickened and smooth. Cook for 1 minute, then season with salt and pepper to taste.

Put the natural yogurt in a serving bowl and sprinkle with a little paprika.

Transfer the beef goulash to a warmed serving dish, garnish with chopped fresh parsley and serve with rice and yogurt.

SERVES 4

2 tbsp vegetable oil

1 large onion, chopped

1 garlic clove, crushed

750 g/1 lb 10 oz lean stewing steak

2 tbsp paprika

425 g/15 oz canned chopped
 tomatoes

2 tbsp tomato purée

1 large red pepper, deseeded and
 chopped

175 g/6 oz mushrooms, sliced

600 ml/1 pint beef stock

1 tbsp cornflour

1 tbsp water

salt and pepper

4 tbsp natural yogurt

paprika, for sprinkling

chopped fresh parsley, to garnish

freshly cooked long-grain and wild
 rice, to serve

Chilli con Carne

Preheat the oven to 160°C/325°F/Gas Mark 3. Using a sharp knife, cut the beef into 2-cm/¾-inch cubes. Heat the vegetable oil in a large flameproof casserole dish and fry the beef over a medium heat until well sealed on all sides. Remove the beef from the casserole with a slotted spoon and reserve until required.

Add the onion and garlic to the casserole and fry until lightly browned; then stir in the flour and cook for 1–2 minutes.

Stir in the tomato juice and tomatoes and bring to the boil. Return the beef to the casserole and add the chilli sauce, cumin and salt and pepper to taste. Cover and cook in the preheated oven for 1½ hours, or until the beef is almost tender.

Stir in the kidney beans, oregano and parsley, and adjust the seasoning to taste, if necessary. Cover the casserole and return to the oven for 45 minutes. Transfer to 4 large, warmed serving plates, garnish with sprigs of fresh herbs and serve immediately with freshly cooked rice and tortillas.

SERVES 4

750 g/1 lb 10 oz lean stewing steak

2 tbsp vegetable oil

1 large onion, sliced

2–4 garlic cloves, crushed

1 tbsp plain flour

425 ml/15 fl oz tomato juice

400 g/14 oz canned tomatoes

1–2 tbsp sweet chilli sauce

1 tsp ground cumin

salt and pepper

425 g/15 oz canned red kidney
   beans, drained and rinsed

½ teaspoon dried oregano

1–2 tbsp chopped fresh parsley

sprigs of fresh herbs, to garnish

freshly cooked rice, to serve

tortillas, to serve

Beef Stroganoff

Place the dried ceps in a bowl and cover with hot water. Leave to soak for 20 minutes. Meanwhile, cut the beef against the grain into 5-mm/¼-inch thick slices, then into 1-cm/½-inch long strips, and reserve.

Drain the mushrooms, reserving the soaking liquid, and chop. Sieve the soaking liquid through a fine-mesh sieve or coffee filter and reserve.

Heat half the oil in a large frying pan. Add the shallots and cook over a low heat, stirring occasionally, for 5 minutes, or until softened. Add the soaked mushrooms, reserved soaking water and whole chestnut mushrooms and cook, stirring frequently, for 10 minutes, or until almost all of the liquid has evaporated, then transfer the mixture to a plate.

Heat the remaining oil in the frying pan, add the beef and cook, stirring frequently, for 4 minutes, or until browned all over. You may need to do this in batches. Return the mushroom mixture to the frying pan and season to taste with salt and pepper. Place the mustard and cream in a small bowl and stir to mix, then fold into the meat and mushroom mixture. Heat through gently, then serve with freshly cooked pasta, garnished with chives.

SERVES 4

15 g/½ oz dried ceps

350 g/12 oz beef fillet

2 tbsp olive oil

115 g/4 oz shallots, sliced

175 g/6 oz chestnut mushrooms

salt and pepper

½ tsp Dijon mustard

5 tbsp double cream

freshly cooked pasta, to serve

fresh chives, to garnish

Beef & Vegetable Stew with Corn

Trim any fat or gristle from the beef and cut into 2.5-cm/1-inch chunks. Mix the flour and spices together. Toss the beef in the spiced flour until well coated.

Heat the oil in a large, heavy-based saucepan and cook the onion, garlic and celery, stirring frequently, for 5 minutes, or until softened. Add the beef and cook over a high heat, stirring frequently, for 3 minutes, or until browned on all sides and sealed.

Add the carrots, then remove from the heat. Gradually stir in the lager and stock, then return to the heat and bring to the boil, stirring. Reduce the heat, cover and simmer, stirring occasionally, for 1¹/₂ hours.

Add the potatoes to the saucepan and simmer for a further 15 minutes. Add the red pepper and corn on the cob and simmer for a further 15 minutes, then add the tomatoes and peas and simmer for a further 10 minutes, or until the beef and vegetables are tender. Season to taste with salt and pepper, stir in the coriander and serve.

SERVES 4

450 g/1 lb braising beef steak

1¹/₂ tbsp plain flour

1 tsp hot paprika

1–1¹/₂ tsp chilli powder

1 tsp ground ginger

2 tbsp olive oil

1 large onion, cut into chunks

3 garlic cloves, sliced

2 celery sticks, sliced

225 g/8 oz carrots, chopped

300 ml/10 fl oz lager

300 ml/10 fl oz beef stock

350 g/12 oz potatoes, chopped

1 red pepper, deseeded and
   chopped

2 corn on the cob, halved

115 g/4 oz tomatoes, quartered

115 g/4 oz shelled fresh or frozen
   peas

salt and pepper

1 tbsp chopped fresh coriander

Pepper Pot-style Stew

Trim any fat or gristle from the beef and cut into 2.5-cm/1-inch chunks. Toss the beef in the flour until well coated and reserve any remaining flour.

Heat the oil in a large, heavy-based saucepan and cook the onion, garlic, chilli and celery with the cloves and allspice, stirring frequently, for 5 minutes, or until softened. Add the beef and cook over a high heat, stirring frequently, for 3 minutes, or until browned on all sides and sealed. Sprinkle in the reserved flour and cook, stirring constantly, for 2 minutes, then remove from the heat.

Add the hot pepper sauce and gradually stir in the stock, then return to the heat and bring to the boil, stirring. Reduce the heat, cover and simmer, stirring occasionally, for $1^1/2$ hours.

Add the squash and red pepper to the saucepan and simmer for a further 15 minutes. Add the tomatoes and okra and simmer for a further 15 minutes, or until the beef is tender. Serve with mixed wild and basmati rice.

SERVES 4

450 g/1 lb braising beef steak

$1^1/2$ tbsp plain flour

2 tbsp olive oil

1 Spanish onion, chopped

3–4 garlic cloves, crushed

1 fresh green chilli, deseeded and chopped

3 celery sticks, sliced

4 whole cloves

1 tsp ground allspice

1–2 teaspoons hot pepper sauce, or to taste

600 ml/1 pint beef stock

225 g/8 oz deseeded and peeled squash, such as acorn, cut into small chunks

1 large red pepper, deseeded and chopped

4 tomatoes, roughly chopped

115 g/4 oz okra, trimmed and halved

mixed wild and basmati rice, to serve

Beef Chop Suey

Combine all the marinade ingredients in a bowl and marinate the beef for at least 20 minutes. Blanch the broccoli in a large pan of boiling water for 30 seconds. Drain and set aside.

In a preheated wok or deep pan, heat 1 tablespoon of the oil and stir-fry the beef until the colour has changed. Remove and set aside. Wipe out the wok or pan with kitchen paper.

In the clean wok or deep pan, heat the remaining oil and stir-fry the onion for 1 minute. Add the celery and broccoli and cook for 2 minutes. Add the mangetout, bamboo shoots, water chestnuts and mushrooms and cook for 1 minute. Add the beef, season with the oyster sauce and salt and serve.

SERVES 4
for the marinade
1 tbsp Shaoxing rice wine
pinch of white pepper
pinch of salt
1 tbsp light soy sauce
$^1/_2$ tsp sesame oil

450 g/1 lb ribeye or sirloin steak, thinly sliced
1 head of broccoli, cut into small florets
2 tbsp vegetable or groundnut oil
1 onion, thinly sliced
2 sticks celery, thinly sliced diagonally
225 g/8 oz mangetout, sliced in half lengthways
55 g/2 oz fresh or canned bamboo shoots, rinsed and julienned (if using fresh shoots, boil in water first for 30 minutes)
8 water chestnuts, thinly sliced
225 g/8 oz mushrooms, thinly sliced
1 tbsp oyster sauce
1 tsp salt

Osso Bucco

Heat the oil and butter in a large, heavy-based frying pan. Add the onions and leek and cook over a low heat, stirring occasionally, for 5 minutes, until softened.

Spread out the flour on a plate and season with salt and pepper. Toss the pieces of veal in the flour to coat, shaking off any excess. Add the veal to the frying pan, increase the heat to high and cook until browned on both sides.

Gradually stir in the wine and stock and bring just to the boil, stirring constantly. Lower the heat, cover and simmer for $1^1/4$ hours, or until the veal is very tender.

Meanwhile, make the gremolata by mixing the parsley, garlic and lemon rind in a small bowl.

Transfer the veal to a warmed serving dish with a slotted spoon. Bring the sauce to the boil and cook, stirring occasionally, until thickened and reduced. Pour the sauce over the veal, sprinkle with the gremolata and serve immediately.

SERVES 4

1 tbsp virgin olive oil

4 tbsp butter

2 onions, chopped

1 leek, sliced

3 tbsp plain flour

salt and pepper

4 thick slices of veal shin (osso bucco)

300 ml/$^1/2$ pint white wine

300 ml/$^1/2$ pint veal or chicken stock

for the gremolata

2 tbsp chopped fresh parsley

1 garlic clove, finely chopped

grated rind of 1 lemon

Lamb Shanks

Dry-fry the coriander and cumin seeds until fragrant, then pound with the cinnamon, chilli and 2 garlic cloves in a mortar and pestle. Stir in half the oil and the lime rind. Rub the spice paste all over the lamb and marinate for 4 hours.

Preheat the oven to 200°C/400°F/Gas Mark 6. Heat the remaining oil in a flameproof casserole and cook the lamb, turning frequently, until evenly browned. Chop the remaining garlic and add to the casserole with the onions, carrots, celery and lime, then pour in enough stock or water to cover. Stir in the tomato paste, add the herbs and season with salt and pepper.

Cover and cook in the preheated oven for 30 minutes. Reduce the oven temperature to 160°C/325°F/Gas Mark 3 and cook for a further 3 hours, or until very tender.

Transfer the lamb to a dish. Strain the cooking liquid to remove any solids, then return the liquid to the casserole. Boil until reduced and thickened. Serve the lamb with the sauce poured over it, garnished with sprigs of rosemary.

SERVES 6

1 tsp coriander seeds

1 tsp cumin seeds

1 tsp ground cinnamon

1 fresh green chilli, deseeded and finely chopped

1 garlic bulb, separated into cloves

125 ml/4 fl oz groundnut or sunflower oil

grated rind of 1 lime

6 lamb shanks

2 onions, chopped

2 carrots, chopped

2 celery sticks, chopped

1 lime, chopped

about 700 ml/1¼ pints beef stock or water

1 tsp sun-dried tomato paste

2 fresh mint sprigs

2 fresh rosemary sprigs, plus extra to garnish

salt and pepper

Irish Stew

Preheat the oven to 160°C/325°F/Gas Mark 3. Spread the flour on a plate and season with salt and pepper. Roll the pieces of lamb in the flour to coat, shaking off any excess, and arrange in the base of a casserole.

Layer the onions, carrots and potatoes on top of the lamb.

Sprinkle in the thyme and pour in the stock, then cover and cook in the preheated oven for $2^{1}/_{2}$ hours. Garnish with the chopped fresh parsley and serve straight from the casserole.

SERVES 4

4 tbsp plain flour

salt and pepper

1.3 kg/3 lb middle neck of lamb, trimmed of visible fat

3 large onions, chopped

3 carrots, sliced

450 g/1 lb potatoes, quartered

$^{1}/_{2}$ tsp dried thyme

850 ml/$1^{1}/_{2}$ pints hot beef stock

2 tbsp chopped fresh parsley, to garnish

Lamb Stew with Chickpeas

Heat 4 tablespoons of the oil in a large, heavy-based flameproof casserole over a medium–high heat. Reduce the heat, add the chorizo and fry for 1 minute. Transfer to a plate. Add the onions to the casserole and fry for 2 minutes, then add the garlic and continue frying for 3 minutes, or until the onions are soft, but not brown. Remove from the casserole and set aside.

Heat the remaining 2 tablespoons of oil in the casserole. Add the lamb cubes in a single layer without over-crowding the casserole, and fry until browned on each side; work in batches, if necessary.

Return the onion mixture and chorizo to the casserole with all the lamb. Stir in the stock, wine, vinegar, tomatoes with their juices and salt and pepper to taste. Bring to the boil, scraping any glazed bits from the base of the casserole. Reduce the heat and stir in the thyme, bay leaves and paprika.

Transfer to a preheated oven, 160°C/325°F/Gas Mark 3, and cook, covered, for 40–45 minutes until the lamb is tender. Stir in the chickpeas and return to the oven, uncovered, for 10 minutes, or until they are heated through and the juices are reduced.

Taste and adjust the seasoning. Serve garnished with thyme.

SERVES 4–6

6 tbsp olive oil

225 g/8 oz chorizo sausage, cut into 5-mm/^{1}/$_4$-inch thick slices, casings removed

2 large onions, chopped

6 large garlic cloves, crushed

900 g/2 lb boned leg of lamb, cut into 5-cm/2-inch chunks

250 ml/9 fl oz lamb stock or water

125 ml/4 fl oz red wine, such as Rioja or Tempranillo

2 tbsp sherry vinegar

800 g/1 lb 12 oz canned chopped tomatoes

salt and pepper

4 sprigs fresh thyme, plus extra to garnish

2 bay leaves

^{1}/$_2$ tsp sweet Spanish paprika

800 g/1 lb 12 oz canned chickpeas, rinsed and drained

Mediterranean Lamb with Apricots & Pistachio Nuts

Put the saffron threads in a heatproof jug with the water and leave for at least 10 minutes to infuse. Trim off any fat or gristle from the lamb and cut into 2.5-cm/1-inch chunks. Mix the flour and spices together, then toss the lamb in the spiced flour until well coated and reserve any remaining spiced flour.

Heat the oil in a large, heavy-based saucepan and cook the onion and garlic, stirring frequently, for 5 minutes, or until softened. Add the lamb and cook over a high heat, stirring frequently, for 3 minutes, or until browned on all sides and sealed. Sprinkle in the reserved spiced flour and cook, stirring constantly, for 2 minutes, then remove from the heat.

Gradually stir in the stock and the saffron and its soaking liquid, then return to the heat and bring to the boil, stirring. Add the cinnamon stick and apricots. Reduce the heat, cover and simmer, stirring occasionally, for 1 hour.

Add the courgettes and tomatoes and cook for a further 15 minutes. Discard the cinnamon stick. Stir in the fresh coriander and season to taste with salt and pepper. Serve sprinkled with the pistachio nuts, accompanied by couscous.

SERVES 4

pinch of saffron threads

2 tbsp almost-boiling water

450 g/1 lb lean, boneless lamb, such as leg steaks

1^{1}/$_{2}$ tbsp plain flour

1 tsp ground coriander

^{1}/$_{2}$ tsp ground cumin

^{1}/$_{2}$ tsp ground allspice

1 tbsp olive oil

1 onion, chopped

2–3 garlic cloves, chopped

450 ml/16 fl oz lamb or chicken stock

1 cinnamon stick, bruised

85 g/3 oz dried apricots, roughly chopped

175 g/6 oz courgettes, sliced

115 g/4 oz cherry tomatoes

1 tbsp chopped fresh coriander

salt and pepper

2 tbsp roughly chopped pistachio nuts, to garnish

couscous, to serve

Cinnamon Lamb Casserole

Season the flour with salt and pepper to taste then put it with the lamb in a polythene bag, hold the top closed and shake until the lamb cubes are lightly coated all over. Remove the lamb from the bag, shake off any excess flour and set aside.

Heat the oil in a large, flameproof casserole and cook the onions and garlic, stirring frequently, for 5 minutes, or until softened. Add the lamb and cook over a high heat, stirring frequently, for 5 minutes, or until browned on all sides and sealed.

Stir the wine, vinegar and tomatoes and their juice into the casserole, scraping any sediment from the base of the casserole, and bring to the boil. Reduce the heat and add the raisins, cinnamon, sugar and bay leaf. Season to taste with salt and pepper. Cover and simmer gently for 2 hours, or until the lamb is tender.

Meanwhile, make the topping. Put the yogurt into a small serving bowl, stir in the garlic and season to taste with salt and pepper. Cover and chill in the refrigerator until required.

Discard the bay leaf and serve hot, topped with a spoonful of the garlicky yogurt and dusted with paprika.

SERVES 6

2 tbsp plain flour

salt and pepper

1 kg/2 lb 4 oz lean boneless lamb, cubed

2 tbsp olive oil

2 large onions, sliced

1 garlic clove, finely chopped

300 ml/10 fl oz full-bodied red wine

2 tbsp red wine vinegar

400 g/14 oz canned chopped tomatoes

55 g/2 oz seedless raisins

1 tbsp ground cinnamon

pinch of sugar

1 bay leaf

salt and pepper

paprika, to garnish

for the topping

150 ml/5 fl oz natural Greek yogurt

2 garlic cloves, crushed

salt and pepper

French Country Casserole

Preheat the oven to 180°C/350°F/Gas Mark 4. Heat the oil in a large, flameproof casserole. Add the lamb in batches and cook over a medium heat, stirring, for 5–8 minutes, or until browned. Transfer to a plate.

Add the sliced leeks to the casserole and cook, stirring occasionally, for 5 minutes, or until softened. Sprinkle in the flour and cook, stirring, for 1 minute. Pour in the wine and stock and bring to the boil, stirring. Stir in the tomato purée, sugar, chopped mint and apricots and season to taste with salt and pepper.

Return the lamb to the casserole and stir. Arrange the potato slices on top and brush with the melted butter. Cover and bake in the preheated oven for 1¹/₂ hours.

Increase the oven temperature to 200°C/400°F/Gas Mark 6, uncover the casserole and bake for a further 30 minutes, or until the potato topping is golden brown. Serve immediately, garnished with fresh mint sprigs.

SERVES 6

2 tbsp sunflower oil

2 kg/4 lb 8 oz boneless leg of lamb, cut into 2.5-cm/1-inch cubes

6 leeks, sliced

1 tbsp plain flour

150 ml/5 fl oz rosé wine

300 ml/10 fl oz chicken stock

1 tbsp tomato purée

1 tbsp sugar

2 tbsp chopped fresh mint

115 g/4 oz dried apricots, chopped

salt and pepper

1 kg/2 lb 4 oz potatoes, sliced

3 tbsp melted unsalted butter

fresh mint sprigs, to garnish

Lamb with Pears

Preheat the oven to 160°C/325°F/Gas Mark 3. Heat the olive oil in a flameproof casserole over a medium heat. Add the lamb and cook, turning frequently, for 5–10 minutes, or until browned on all sides.

Arrange the pear quarters on top, then sprinkle over the ginger. Cover with the potatoes. Pour in the cider and season to taste with salt and pepper. Cover and cook in the preheated oven for 1¼ hours.

Trim the stalk ends of the green beans. Remove the casserole from the oven and add the beans, then re-cover and return to the oven for a further 30 minutes. Taste and adjust the seasoning. Sprinkle with the chives and serve.

SERVES 4

1 tbsp olive oil

1 kg/2 lb 4 oz best end-of-neck lamb cutlets, trimmed of visible fat

6 pears, peeled, cored and quartered

1 tsp ground ginger

4 potatoes, diced

4 tbsp dry cider

salt and pepper

450 g/1 lb green beans

2 tbsp snipped fresh chives, to garnish

Azerbaijani Lamb Pilau

Heat the oil in a large flameproof casserole or saucepan over a high heat. Add the lamb, in batches, and cook over a high heat, turning frequently, for 7 minutes, or until lightly browned.

Add the onions, reduce the heat to medium and cook for 2 minutes, or until beginning to soften. Add the cumin and rice and cook, stirring to coat, for 2 minutes, or until the rice is translucent. Stir in the tomato purée and the saffron threads.

Add the pomegranate juice and stock. Bring to the boil, stirring. Stir in the apricots and raisins. Reduce the heat to low, cover, and simmer for 20–25 minutes, or until the lamb and rice are tender and all of the liquid has been absorbed.

Season to taste with salt and pepper, then sprinkle the shredded mint and watercress over the pilau and serve straight from the casserole.

SERVES 4

2–3 tbsp vegetable oil

650 g/1 lb 7 oz boneless lamb shoulder, cut into 2.5-cm/1-inch cubes

2 onions, roughly chopped

1 tsp ground cumin

200 g/7 oz arborio rice

1 tbsp tomato purée

1 tsp saffron threads

100 ml/3½ fl oz pomegranate juice

850 ml/1½ pints lamb stock, chicken stock or water

115 g/4 oz no-soak dried apricots or prunes, halved

2 tbsp raisins

salt and pepper

2 tbsp shredded fresh mint

2 tbsp shredded fresh watercress

Pot-roast Pork

Heat the oil with half the butter in a heavy-based saucepan or flameproof casserole. Add the pork and cook over a medium heat, turning frequently, for 5–10 minutes, or until browned. Transfer to a plate.

Add the shallots to the saucepan and cook, stirring frequently, for 5 minutes, or until softened. Add the juniper berries and thyme sprigs and return the pork to the saucepan, with any juices that have collected on the plate. Pour in the cider and stock, season to taste with salt and pepper, then cover and simmer for 30 minutes. Turn the pork over and add the celery. Re-cover the pan and cook for a further 40 minutes.

Meanwhile, make a beurre manié by mashing the remaining butter with the flour in a small bowl. Transfer the pork and celery to a platter with a slotted spoon and keep warm. Remove and discard the juniper berries and thyme. Whisk the beurre manié, a little at a time, into the simmering cooking liquid. Cook, stirring constantly, for 2 minutes, then stir in the cream and bring to the boil.

Slice the pork and spoon a little of the sauce over it. Garnish with thyme sprigs and serve immediately with the celery, peas and remaining sauce.

SERVES 4

1 tbsp sunflower oil

55 g/2 oz butter

1 kg/2 lb 4 oz boned and
    rolled pork loin joint

4 shallots, chopped

6 juniper berries

2 fresh thyme sprigs, plus extra
    to garnish

150 ml/5 fl oz dry cider

150 ml/5 fl oz chicken stock
    or water

salt and pepper

8 celery sticks, chopped

2 tbsp plain flour

150 ml/5 fl oz double cream

freshly cooked peas, to serve

Pork & Vegetable Ragout

Trim off any fat or gristle from the pork and cut into thin strips about 5 cm/2 inch long. Mix the flour and spices together. Toss the pork in the spiced flour until well coated and reserve any remaining spiced flour.

Heat the oil in a large, heavy-based saucepan and cook the onion, stirring frequently, for 5 minutes, or until softened. Add the pork and cook over a high heat, stirring frequently, for 5 minutes, or until browned on all sides and sealed. Sprinkle in the reserved spiced flour and cook, stirring constantly, for 2 minutes, then remove from the heat.

Gradually stir the tomatoes to the saucepan. Blend the tomato purée with a little of the stock in a jug and gradually stir into the saucepan, then stir in half the remaining stock.

Add the carrots, then return to the heat and bring to the boil, stirring. Reduce the heat, cover and simmer, stirring occasionally, for 1^1/$_2$ hours. Add the squash and cook for a further 15 minutes.

Add the leeks and okra, and the remaining stock if you prefer a thinner ragout. Simmer for a further 15 minutes, or until the pork and vegetables are tender. Season to taste with salt and pepper, then garnish with fresh parsley and serve with couscous.

SERVES 4

450 g/1 lb lean boneless pork

1^1/$_2$ tbsp plain flour

1 tsp ground coriander

1 tsp ground cumin

1^1/$_2$ tsp ground cinnamon

1 tbsp olive oil

1 onion, chopped

400 g/14 oz canned chopped tomatoes

2 tbsp tomato purée

300–450 ml/10–16 fl oz chicken stock

225 g/8 oz carrots, chopped

350 g/12 oz squash, such as kabocha, peeled, deseeded and chopped

225 g/8 oz leeks, sliced, blanched and drained

115 g/4 oz okra, trimmed and sliced

salt and pepper

fresh parsley sprigs, to garnish

couscous, to serve

Pork with Red Cabbage

Preheat the oven to 160°C/325°F/Gas Mark 3. Heat the oil in a flameproof casserole. Add the pork and cook over a medium heat, turning frequently, for 5–10 minutes, or until browned. Transfer to a plate.

Add the chopped onion to the casserole and cook over a low heat, stirring occasionally, for 5 minutes, or until softened. Add the cabbage, in batches, and cook, stirring, for 2 minutes. Transfer each batch (mixed with some onion) into a bowl with a slotted spoon.

Add the apple slices, cloves and sugar to the bowl and mix well, then place about half the mixture in the base of the casserole. Top with the pork and add the remaining cabbage mixture. Sprinkle in the lemon juice and add the strip of rind. Cover and cook in the preheated oven for 1^1/$_2$ hours.

Transfer the pork to a plate. Transfer the cabbage mixture to the plate with a slotted spoon and keep warm. Bring the cooking juices to the boil over a high heat and reduce slightly. Slice the pork and arrange on warmed serving plates, surrounded with the cabbage mixture. Spoon the cooking juices over the meat and serve with wedges of lemon.

SERVES 4

1 tbsp sunflower oil

750 g/1 lb 10 oz boned and rolled pork loin joint

1 onion, finely chopped

500 g/1 lb 2 oz red cabbage, thick stems removed and leaves shredded

2 large cooking apples, peeled, cored and sliced

3 cloves

1 tsp brown sugar

3 tbsp lemon juice, and a thinly pared strip of lemon rind

lemon wedges, to garnish

Paprika Pork

Cut the pork into 4-cm/ 1$\frac{1}{2}$-inch cubes. Heat the oil and butter in a large saucepan. Add the pork and cook over a medium heat, stirring, for 5 minutes, or until browned. Transfer to a plate with a slotted spoon.

Add the chopped onion to the saucepan and cook, stirring occasionally, for 5 minutes, or until softened. Stir in the paprika and flour and cook, stirring constantly, for 2 minutes. Gradually stir in the stock and bring to the boil, stirring constantly.

Return the pork to the saucepan, add the sherry and sliced mushrooms and season to taste with salt and pepper. Cover and simmer gently for 20 minutes, or until the pork is tender. Stir in the soured cream and serve.

SERVES 4

675 g/1 lb 8 oz pork fillet

2 tbsp sunflower oil

25 g/1 oz butter

1 onion, chopped

1 tbsp paprika

25 g/1 oz plain flour

300 ml/10 fl oz chicken stock

4 tbsp dry sherry

115 g/4 oz mushrooms, sliced

salt and pepper

150 ml/5 fl oz soured cream

Pork Chops with Peppers & Sweetcorn

Heat the oil in a large, flameproof casserole. Add the pork chops in batches and cook over a medium heat, turning occasionally, for 5 minutes, or until browned. Transfer the chops to a plate with a slotted spoon.

Add the chopped onion to the casserole and cook, stirring occasionally, for 5 minutes, or until softened. Add the garlic and peppers and cook, stirring occasionally for a further 5 minutes. Stir in the sweetcorn kernels and their juices, the parsley and season to taste with salt and pepper.

Return the chops to the casserole, spooning the vegetable mixture over them. Cover and simmer for 30 minutes, or until tender. Serve immediately with mashed potatoes.

SERVES 4

1 tbsp sunflower oil

4 pork chops, trimmed of visible fat

1 onion, chopped

1 garlic clove, finely chopped

1 green pepper, deseeded and sliced

1 red pepper, deseeded and sliced

325 g/11^1/$_2$ oz canned sweetcorn kernels

1 tbsp chopped fresh parsley

salt and pepper

mashed potatoes, to serve

Sausage & Bean Casserole

Prick the sausages all over with a fork. Heat 2 tablespoons of the oil in a large, heavy frying pan. Add the sausages and cook over low heat, turning frequently, for 10–15 minutes, until evenly browned and cooked through. Remove them from the frying pan and keep warm. Drain off the oil and wipe out the pan with kitchen paper.

Heat the remaining oil in the frying pan. Add the onion, garlic and pepper to the frying pan and cook for 5 minutes, stirring occasionally, or until softened.

Add the tomatoes to the frying pan and leave the mixture to simmer for about 5 minutes, stirring occasionally, or until slightly reduced and thickened.

Stir the sun-dried tomato paste, cannellini beans and Italian sausages into the mixture in the frying pan. Cook for 4–5 minutes or until the mixture is piping hot. Add 4–5 tablespoons of water, if the mixture becomes too dry during cooking.

Transfer the Italian sausage and bean casserole to serving plates and serve with mashed potatoes or cooked rice.

SERVES 4

8 Italian sausages

3 tbsp olive oil

1 large onion, chopped

2 garlic cloves, chopped

1 green bell pepper, deseeded and sliced

225g/8 oz fresh tomatoes, skinned and chopped or 400 g/14 oz can tomatoes, chopped

2 tbsp sun-dried tomato paste

400 g/14 oz canned cannellini beans

mashed potatoes or rice, to serve

Pork Oriental

Trim off any fat or gristle from the pork and cut into 2.5-cm/1-inch chunks. Toss the pork in the flour until well coated and reserve any remaining flour.

Heat the oil in a large, heavy-based saucepan and cook the onion, garlic and ginger, stirring frequently, for 5 minutes, or until softened. Add the pork and cook over a high heat, stirring frequently, for 5 minutes, or until browned on all sides and sealed. Sprinkle in the reserved flour and cook, stirring constantly, for 2 minutes, then remove from the heat.

Blend the tomato purée with the stock in a heatproof jug and gradually stir into the saucepan. Drain the pineapple, reserving both the fruit and juice, and stir the juice into the saucepan.

Add the soy sauce to the saucepan, then return to the heat and bring to the boil, stirring. Reduce the heat, cover and simmer, stirring occasionally, for 1 hour. Add the peppers and cook for a further 15 minutes, or until the pork is tender. Stir in the vinegar and the pineapple and heat through for 5 minutes. Serve sprinkled with the spring onions.

SERVES 4

450 g/1 lb lean boneless pork

1^{1}/$_{2}$ tbsp plain flour

1–2 tbsp olive oil

1 onion, cut into small wedges

2–3 garlic cloves, chopped

2.5-cm/1-inch piece fresh root ginger, peeled and grated

1 tbsp tomato purée

300 ml/10 fl oz chicken stock

225 g/8 oz canned pineapple chunks in natural juice

1–1^{1}/$_{2}$ tbsp dark soy sauce

1 red pepper, deseeded and sliced

1 green pepper, deseeded and sliced

1^{1}/$_{2}$ tbsp balsamic vinegar

4 spring onions, diagonally sliced, to garnish

Red Curry Pork with Peppers

Heat the oil in a wok or large frying pan and fry the onion and garlic for 1–2 minutes, until they are softened but not browned.

Add the pork slices and stir-fry for 2–3 minutes until browned all over. Add the pepper, mushrooms and curry paste.

Dissolve the coconut in the stock and add to the wok with the soy sauce. Bring to the boil and simmer for 4–5 minutes until the liquid has reduced and thickened.

Add the tomatoes and coriander and cook for 1–2 minutes before serving with noodles or rice.

SERVES 4

2 tbsp vegetable or groundnut oil

1 onion, roughly chopped

2 garlic cloves, chopped

450 g/1 lb pork fillet, sliced thickly

1 red pepper, deseeded and cut into squares

175 g/6 oz mushrooms, quartered

2 tbsp Thai red curry paste

115 g/4 oz creamed coconut, chopped

300 ml/$\frac{1}{2}$ pint pork or vegetable stock

2 tbsp Thai soy sauce

4 tomatoes, peeled, deseeded and chopped

handful of fresh coriander, chopped

boiled noodles or rice, to serve

Poultry Pot Wonders

One-pot cooking is the perfect technique for poultry, especially chicken, which can sometimes be disappointingly bland and dry when cooked in other ways. Fabulous stews and aromatic curries burst with flavour, and there's even an all-in-one roast chicken with all the classic flavours and none of the classic hassle. Discover the versatility of poultry and explore the ease of one-pot cooking with these inspiring international recipes for chicken, turkey and duck.

Chicken & Barley Stew

Heat the oil in a large pot over a medium heat. Add the chicken and cook for 3 minutes, then turn over and cook on the other side for a further 2 minutes. Add the stock, barley, potatoes, carrots, leek, shallots, tomato purée and bay leaf. Bring to the boil, lower the heat and simmer for 30 minutes.

Add the courgette and chopped parsley, cover the pan and cook for a further 20 minutes, or until the chicken is cooked through. Remove the bay leaf and discard.

In a separate bowl, mix the flour with 4 tablespoons of water and stir into a smooth paste. Add it to the stew and cook, stirring, over a low heat for a further 5 minutes. Season to taste with salt and pepper.

Remove from the heat, ladle into individual serving bowls and garnish with sprigs of fresh parsley. Serve with fresh crusty bread.

SERVES 4

2 tbsp vegetable oil

8 small, skinless chicken thighs

500 ml/18 fl oz chicken stock

100 g/3^1/$_2$ oz pearl barley, rinsed and drained

200 g/7 oz small new potatoes, scrubbed and halved lengthways

2 large carrots, peeled and sliced

1 leek, trimmed and sliced

2 shallots, sliced

1 tbsp tomato purée

1 bay leaf

1 courgette, trimmed and sliced

2 tbsp chopped fresh flat-leaf parsley, plus extra sprigs to garnish

2 tbsp plain flour

salt and pepper

fresh crusty bread, to serve

Coq au Vin

Melt half the butter with the olive oil in a large, flameproof casserole. Add the chicken and cook over a medium heat, stirring, for 8–10 minutes, or until golden brown all over. Add the bacon, onions, mushrooms and garlic.

Pour in the brandy and set it alight with a match or taper. When the flames have died down, add the wine, stock and bouquet garni and season to taste with salt and pepper. Bring to the boil, reduce the heat and simmer gently for 1 hour, or until the chicken pieces are cooked through and tender. Meanwhile, make a beurre manié by mashing the remaining butter with the flour in a small bowl.

Remove and discard the bouquet garni. Transfer the chicken to a large plate and keep warm. Stir the beurre manié into the casserole, a little at a time. Bring to the boil, return the chicken to the casserole and serve immediately, garnished with bay leaves.

SERVES 4

55 g/2 oz butter

2 tbsp olive oil

1.8 kg/4 lb chicken pieces

115 g/4 oz rindless smoked bacon, cut into strips

115 g/4 oz baby onions

115 g/4 oz chestnut mushrooms, halved

2 garlic cloves, finely chopped

2 tbsp brandy

225 ml/8 fl oz red wine

300 ml/10 fl oz chicken stock

1 bouquet garni

salt and pepper

2 tbsp plain flour

bay leaves, to garnish

Italian-style Roast Chicken

Preheat the oven to 190°C/375°F/Gas Mark 5. Rinse the chicken inside and out with cold water and drain well. Carefully cut between the skin and the top of the breast meat using a small pointed knife. Slide a finger into the slit and carefully enlarge it to form a pocket. Continue until the skin is completely lifted away from both breasts and the top of the legs.

Chop the leaves from 3 rosemary stems. Mix with the feta cheese, sun-dried tomato paste, butter and pepper to taste, then spoon under the skin. Put the chicken in a large roasting tin, cover with foil and cook in the preheated oven, for 20 minutes per 500 g/1 lb 2 oz, plus 20 minutes.

Break the garlic bulb into cloves but do not peel. Add the vegetables and garlic to the chicken after 40 minutes.

Drizzle with oil, tuck in a few stems of rosemary and season with salt and pepper. Cook for the remaining calculated time, removing the foil for the last 40 minutes to brown the chicken.

Transfer the chicken to a serving platter. Place some of the vegetables around the chicken and transfer the remainder to a warmed serving dish. Spoon the fat out of the roasting tin (it will be floating on top) and stir the flour into the remaining cooking juices. Place the roasting tin on top of the hob and cook over medium heat for 2 minutes, then gradually stir in the stock. Bring to the boil, stirring until thickened. Strain into a gravy boat and serve with the chicken.

SERVES 6

2.5 kg/5 lb 8 oz chicken

fresh rosemary sprigs

175 g/6 oz feta cheese, coarsely grated

2 tbsp sun-dried tomato paste

60 g/2 oz butter, softened

salt and pepper

1 bulb garlic

1 kg/2 lb 4 oz new potatoes, halved if large

1 each red, green and yellow pepper, deseeded and cut into chunks

3 courgettes, thinly sliced

2 tbsp olive oil

2 tbsp plain flour

600 ml/1 pint chicken stock

Spicy Aromatic Chicken

Rub the chicken pieces with the lemon. Heat the oil in a large flameproof casserole or lidded frying pan. Add the onion and garlic and fry for 5 minutes, until softened. Add the chicken pieces and fry for 5–10 minutes, until browned on all sides.

Pour in the wine and add the tomatoes with their juice, the sugar, cinnamon, cloves, allspice, salt and pepper and bring to the boil. Cover the casserole and simmer for 45 minutes–1 hour, until the chicken is tender.

Meanwhile, if using artichoke hearts, cut them in half. Add the artichokes or okra and the olives to the casserole 10 minutes before the end of cooking, and continue to simmer until heated through. Serve hot.

SERVES 4

4–8 chicken pieces, skinned

$^1/_2$ lemon, cut into wedges

4 tbsp olive oil

1 onion, roughly chopped

2 large garlic cloves, finely chopped

125 ml/4 fl oz dry white wine

400 g/14 oz canned chopped
 tomatoes in juice

pinch of sugar

$^1/_2$ tsp ground cinnamon

$^1/_2$ tsp ground cloves

$^1/_2$ tsp ground allspice

salt and pepper

400g/14 oz canned artichoke hearts
 or okra, drained

8 black olives, stoned

Brunswick Stew

Season the chicken pieces with salt and dust with paprika.

Heat the oil and butter in a flameproof casserole or large saucepan. Add the chicken pieces and cook over a medium heat, turning, for 10–15 minutes, or until golden. Transfer to a plate with a slotted spoon.

Add the onion and peppers to the casserole. Cook over a low heat, stirring occasionally, for 5 minutes, or until softened. Add the tomatoes, wine, stock, Worcestershire sauce, Tabasco sauce and parsley and bring to the boil, stirring. Return the chicken to the casserole, cover and simmer, stirring occasionally, for 30 minutes.

Add the sweetcorn and beans to the casserole, partially re-cover and simmer for a further 30 minutes. Place the flour and water in a small bowl and mix to make a paste. Stir a ladleful of the cooking liquid into the paste, then stir it into the stew. Cook, stirring frequently, for 5 minutes. Serve, garnished with parsley.

SERVES 6

1.8 kg/4 lb chicken pieces

salt

2 tbsp paprika

2 tbsp olive oil

25 g/1 oz butter

450 g/1 lb onions, chopped

2 yellow peppers, deseeded and chopped

400 g/14 oz canned chopped tomatoes

225 ml/8 fl oz dry white wine

450 ml/16 fl oz chicken stock

1 tbsp Worcestershire sauce

$1/2$ tsp Tabasco sauce

1 tbsp finely chopped fresh parsley

325 g/11$1/2$ oz canned sweetcorn kernels, drained

425 g/15 oz canned butter beans, drained and rinsed

2 tbsp plain flour

4 tbsp water

fresh parsley sprigs, to garnish

Chicken in White Wine

Preheat the oven to 160°C/325°F/Gas Mark 3. Melt half the butter with the oil in a flameproof casserole. Add the bacon and cook over a medium heat, stirring, for 5–10 minutes, or until golden brown. Transfer the bacon to a large plate. Add the onions and garlic to the casserole and cook over a low heat, stirring occasionally, for 10 minutes, or until golden. Transfer to the plate. Add the chicken and cook over a medium heat, stirring constantly, for 8–10 minutes, or until golden. Transfer to the plate.

Drain off any excess fat from the casserole. Stir in the wine and stock and bring to the boil, scraping any sediment off the base. Add the bouquet garni and season to taste. Return the bacon, onions and chicken to the casserole. Cover and cook in the preheated oven for 1 hour. Add the mushrooms, re-cover and cook for 15 minutes. Meanwhile, make a beurre manié by mashing the remaining butter with the flour in a small bowl.

Remove the casserole from the oven and set over a medium heat. Remove and discard the bouquet garni. Whisk in the beurre manié, a little at a time. Bring to the boil, stirring constantly, then serve, garnished with fresh herb sprigs.

SERVES 4

55 g/2 oz butter

2 tbsp olive oil

2 rindless, thick streaky bacon rashers, chopped

115 g/4 oz baby onions, peeled

1 garlic clove, finely chopped

1.8 kg/4 lb chicken pieces

400 ml/14 fl oz dry white wine

300 ml/10 fl oz chicken stock

1 bouquet garni

salt and pepper

115 g/4 oz button mushrooms

25 g/1 oz plain flour

fresh mixed herbs, to garnish

Hunter's Chicken

Preheat the oven to 160°C/325°F/Gas Mark 3. Heat the butter and oil in a flameproof casserole and cook the chicken over a medium–high heat, turning frequently, for 10 minutes, or until golden all over and sealed. Using a slotted spoon, transfer to a plate.

Add the onions and garlic to the casserole and cook over a low heat, stirring occasionally, for 10 minutes, or until softened and golden. Add the tomatoes with their juice, the herbs, sun-dried tomato paste and wine, and season to taste with salt and pepper. Bring to the boil, then return the chicken portions to the casserole, pushing them down into the sauce.

Cover and cook in the preheated oven for 50 minutes. Add the mushrooms and cook for a further 10 minutes, or until the chicken is tender and the juices run clear when a skewer is inserted into the thickest part of the meat. Serve immediately.

SERVES 4

15 g/^{1}/$_2$ oz unsalted butter

2 tbsp olive oil

1.8 kg/4 lb skinned, unboned chicken portions

2 red onions, sliced

2 garlic cloves, finely chopped

400 g/14 oz canned chopped tomatoes

2 tbsp chopped fresh flat-leaf parsley

6 fresh basil leaves, torn

1 tbsp sun-dried tomato paste

150 ml/5 fl oz red wine

salt and pepper

225 g/8 oz mushrooms, sliced

Florida Chicken

Lightly rinse the chicken and pat dry with kitchen paper. Cut into bite-sized pieces. Season the flour well with salt and pepper. Toss the chicken in the seasoned flour until well coated and reserve any remaining seasoned flour.

Heat the oil in a large, heavy-based frying pan and cook the chicken over a high heat, stirring frequently, for 5 minutes, or until golden on all sides and sealed. Using a slotted spoon, transfer the chicken to a plate.

Add the onion and celery to the frying pan and cook over a medium heat, stirring frequently, for 5 minutes, or until softened. Sprinkle in the reserved seasoned flour and cook, stirring constantly, for 2 minutes, then remove from the heat. Gradually stir in the orange juice, stock, soy sauce and honey, followed by the orange rind, then return to the heat and bring to the boil, stirring.

Return the chicken to the frying pan. Reduce the heat, cover and simmer, stirring occasionally, for 15 minutes. Add the orange pepper, courgettes and corn on the cob and simmer for a further 10 minutes, or until the chicken and vegetables are tender. Add the orange segments, stir well and heat through for 1 minute. Serve garnished with the parsley.

SERVES 4

450 g/1 lb skinless, boneless chicken

$1^1/_2$ tbsp plain flour

salt and pepper

1 tbsp olive oil

1 onion, cut into wedges

2 celery sticks, sliced

150 ml/5 fl oz orange juice

300 ml/10 fl oz chicken stock

1 tbsp light soy sauce

1–2 tsp clear honey

1 tbsp grated orange rind

1 orange pepper, deseeded and chopped

225 g/8 oz courgettes, sliced into half moons

2 small corn on the cob, halved, or 100 g/$3^1/_2$ oz baby sweetcorn

1 orange, peeled and segmented

1 tbsp chopped fresh parsley, to garnish

Thai Green Chicken Curry

First make the curry paste. Deseed the chillies if you like and roughly chop. Place all the paste ingredients except the oil in a mortar and pound with a pestle. Alternatively, process in a food processor. Gradually blend in the oil.

Heat 2 tablespoons of oil in a preheated wok or large, heavy-based frying pan. Add 2 tablespoons of the curry paste and stir-fry briefly until all the aromas are released.

Add the chicken, lime leaves and lemon grass and stir-fry for 3–4 minutes, until the meat is beginning to colour. Add the coconut milk and aubergines and simmer gently for 8–10 minutes, or until tender.

Stir in the fish sauce and serve immediately, garnished with Thai basil sprigs and lime leaves.

SERVES 4

2 tbsp groundnut or sunflower oil

500 g/1 lb 2 oz skinless boneless chicken breasts, cut into cubes

2 kaffir lime leaves, roughly torn

1 lemon grass stalk, finely chopped

225 ml/8 fl oz canned coconut milk

16 baby aubergines, halved

2 tbsp Thai fish sauce

fresh Thai basil sprigs, to garnish

kaffir lime leaves, thinly sliced, to garnish

for the green curry paste

16 fresh green chillies

2 shallots, sliced

4 kaffir lime leaves

1 lemon grass stalk, chopped

2 garlic cloves, chopped

1 tsp cumin seeds

1 tsp coriander seeds

1 tbsp grated fresh root ginger or galangal

1 tsp grated lime rind

5 black peppercorns

1 tbsp sugar

salt

2 tbsp groundnut or sunflower oil

Chicken Tagine

Heat the oil in a large saucepan over a medium heat, add the onion and garlic and cook for 3 minutes, stirring frequently. Add the chicken and cook, stirring constantly, for a further 5 minutes, or until sealed on all sides. Add the cumin and cinnamon sticks to the saucepan halfway through sealing the chicken.

Sprinkle in the flour and cook, stirring constantly, for 2 minutes.

Add the aubergine, red pepper and mushrooms and cook for a further 2 minutes, stirring constantly.

Blend the tomato purée with the stock, stir into the saucepan and bring to the boil. Reduce the heat and add the chickpeas and apricots. Cover and simmer for 15–20 minutes, or until the chicken is tender.

Season with salt and pepper to taste and serve immediately, sprinkled with coriander.

SERVES 4

1 tbsp olive oil

1 onion, cut into small wedges

2–4 garlic cloves, sliced

450 g/1 lb skinless, boneless chicken breast, diced

1 tsp ground cumin

2 cinnamon sticks, lightly bruised

1 tbsp plain wholemeal flour

225 g/8 oz aubergine, diced

1 red pepper, deseeded and chopped

85 g/3 oz button mushrooms, sliced

1 tbsp tomato purée

600 ml/1 pint chicken stock

280 g/10 oz canned chickpeas, drained and rinsed

55 g/2 oz no-soak dried apricots, chopped

salt and pepper

1 tbsp chopped fresh coriander, to garnish

Chicken Jalfrezi

Grind the cumin and coriander seeds in a mortar with a pestle, then reserve. Heat the mustard oil in a large, heavy-based frying pan over a high heat for 1 minute, or until it begins to smoke. Add the vegetable oil, reduce the heat and add the onion and garlic. Cook for 10 minutes, or until golden.

Add the tomato purée, chopped tomatoes, turmeric, ground cumin and coriander seeds, chilli powder, garam masala and vinegar to the frying pan. Stir the mixture until fragrant.

Add the red pepper and broad beans and stir for a further 2 minutes, or until the pepper is softened. Stir in the chicken, and season to taste with salt. Simmer gently for 6–8 minutes, or until the chicken is heated through and the beans are tender. Transfer to warmed serving bowls, garnish with coriander sprigs and serve with freshly cooked rice.

SERVES 4

$^1/_2$ tsp cumin seeds

$^1/_2$ tsp coriander seeds

1 tsp mustard oil

3 tbsp vegetable oil

1 large onion, finely chopped

3 garlic cloves, crushed

1 tbsp tomato purée

2 tomatoes, peeled and chopped

1 tsp ground turmeric

$^1/_2$ tsp chilli powder

$^1/_2$ tsp garam masala

1 tsp red wine vinegar

1 small red pepper, deseeded and chopped

125 g/4$^1/_2$ oz frozen broad beans

500 g/1 lb 2 oz cooked chicken, chopped

salt

fresh coriander sprigs, to garnish

freshly cooked rice, to serve

Balti Chicken

Heat the ghee in a large, heavy-based frying pan. Add the onions and cook over a low heat, stirring occasionally, for 10 minutes, or until golden. Add the sliced tomatoes, kalonji seeds, peppercorns, cardamoms, cinnamon stick, chilli powder, garam masala, garlic paste and ginger paste, and season with salt to taste. Cook, stirring constantly, for 5 minutes.

Add the chicken and cook, stirring constantly, for 5 minutes, or until well coated in the spice paste. Stir in the yogurt. Cover and simmer, stirring occasionally, for 10 minutes.

Stir in the chopped coriander, chillies and lime juice. Transfer to a warmed serving dish, sprinkle with more chopped coriander and serve immediately.

SERVES 6

3 tbsp ghee or vegetable oil

2 large onions, sliced

3 tomatoes, sliced

$^{1}/_{2}$ tsp kalonji seeds

4 black peppercorns

2 cardamom pods

1 cinnamon stick

1 tsp chilli powder

1 tsp garam masala

1 tsp garlic paste

1 tsp ginger paste

salt

700 g/1 lb 9 oz skinless, boneless chicken breasts or thighs, diced

2 tbsp natural yogurt

2 tbsp chopped fresh coriander, plus extra to garnish

2 fresh green chillies, deseeded and finely chopped

2 tbsp lime juice

Chicken with Garlic

Sift the flour onto a large plate and season with paprika and salt and pepper to taste. Dredge the chicken pieces with the flour on both sides, shaking off the excess.

Heat 4 tablespoons of the oil in a large, deep frying pan or flameproof casserole over a medium heat. Add the garlic and fry, stirring frequently, for about 2 minutes to flavour the oil. Remove with a slotted spoon and set aside to drain on kitchen paper.

Add as many chicken pieces, skin-side down, as will fit in a single layer. (Work in batches if necessary, to avoid over-crowding the frying pan, adding a little extra oil if necessary.) Fry for 5 minutes until the skin is golden brown. Turn over and fry for 5 minutes longer.

Pour off any excess oil. Return the garlic and chicken pieces to the frying pan and add the chicken stock, wine and herbs. Bring to the boil, then reduce the heat, cover and simmer for 20–25 minutes until the chicken is cooked through and tender and the garlic is very soft.

Transfer the chicken pieces to a serving platter and keep warm. Bring the cooking liquid to the boil, with the garlic and herbs, and boil until reduced to about 300 ml/½ pint. Remove and discard the cooked herbs. Taste and adjust the seasoning, if necessary.

Spoon the sauce and the garlic cloves over the chicken pieces. Garnish with fresh parsley and thyme, and serve.

SERVES 4

4 tbsp plain flour

Spanish paprika, either hot or smoked sweet, to taste

salt and pepper

1 large chicken, about 1.75 kg/ 3 lb 12 oz, cut into 8 pieces, rinsed and patted dry

4–6 tbsp olive oil

24 large garlic cloves, peeled and halved

450 ml/³/4 pint chicken stock, preferably home-made

4 tbsp dry white wine, such as white Rioja

2 sprigs of fresh flat-leaf parsley, 1 bay leaf and 1 sprig of fresh thyme, tied together

fresh flat-leaf parsley and thyme leaves, to garnish

Louisiana Chicken

Heat the oil in a large, heavy-based saucepan or flameproof casserole. Add the chicken and cook over a medium heat, stirring, for 5–10 minutes, or until golden. Transfer the chicken to a plate with a slotted spoon.

Stir the flour into the oil and cook over a very low heat, stirring constantly, for 15 minutes, or until light golden. Do not let it burn. Immediately, add the onion, celery and green pepper and cook, stirring constantly, for 2 minutes. Add the garlic, thyme and chillies and cook, stirring, for 1 minute.

Stir in the tomatoes and their juices, then gradually stir in the stock. Return the chicken pieces to the saucepan, cover and simmer for 45 minutes, or until the chicken is cooked through and tender. Season to taste with salt and pepper, transfer to warmed serving plates and serve immediately, garnished with some lettuce leaves and a sprinkling of chopped thyme.

SERVES 4

5 tbsp sunflower oil

4 chicken portions

55 g/2 oz plain flour

1 onion, chopped

2 celery sticks, sliced

1 green pepper, deseeded and chopped

2 garlic cloves, finely chopped

2 tsp chopped fresh thyme

2 fresh red chillies, deseeded and finely chopped

400 g/14 oz canned chopped tomatoes

300 ml/10 fl oz chicken stock

salt and pepper

lamb's lettuce, to garnish

chopped fresh thyme, to garnish

Chicken Pepperonata

Toss the chicken thighs in the flour, shaking off the excess.

Heat the oil in a wide frying pan and fry the chicken quickly until sealed and lightly browned, then remove from the pan.

Add the onion to the pan and gently fry until soft. Add the garlic, peppers, tomatoes and oregano, then bring to the boil, stirring.

Arrange the chicken over the vegetables, season well with salt and pepper, then cover the pan tightly and simmer for 20–25 minutes or until the chicken is completely cooked and tender.

Taste and adjust the seasoning if necessary, garnish with oregano and serve with crusty wholemeal bread.

SERVES 4

8 skinless chicken thighs

2 tbsp wholemeal flour

2 tbsp olive oil

1 small onion, thinly sliced

1 garlic clove, crushed

1 each large red, yellow and green peppers, deseeded and thinly sliced

400 g / 14 oz canned chopped tomatoes

1 tbsp chopped oregano, plus extra to garnish

salt and pepper

crusty wholemeal bread, to serve

Chicken Risotto with Saffron

Heat 55 g/2 oz of the butter in a deep saucepan. Add the chicken and onion and cook, stirring frequently, for 8 minutes, or until golden brown.

Add the rice and mix to coat in the butter. Cook, stirring constantly for 2–3 minutes, or until the grains are translucent. Add the wine and cook, stirring constantly, for 1 minute until reduced.

Mix the saffron with 4 tablespoons of the hot stock. Add the liquid to the rice and cook, stirring constantly, until it is absorbed.

Gradually add the remaining hot stock, a ladle at a time. Stir constantly and add more liquid as the rice absorbs each addition. Cook for 20 minutes, or until all the liquid is absorbed and the rice is creamy. Season to taste.

Remove the risotto from the heat and add the remaining butter. Mix well, then stir in the Parmesan until it melts. Spoon the risotto onto warmed plates and serve immediately.

SERVES 4

125 g/4$\frac{1}{2}$ oz butter

900 g/2 lb skinless, boneless chicken breasts, thinly sliced

1 large onion, chopped

500 g/1 lb 2 oz risotto rice

150 ml/5 fl oz white wine

1 tsp crumbled saffron threads

1.3 litres/2$\frac{1}{4}$ pints chicken stock

salt and pepper

55 g/2 oz freshly grated Parmesan cheese

Mexican Turkey

Preheat the oven to 160°C/325°F/Gas Mark 3. Spread the flour on a plate and season with salt and pepper. Coat the turkey fillets in the seasoned flour, shaking off any excess. Reserve the seasoned flour.

Heat the oil in a flameproof casserole. Add the turkey fillets and cook over a medium heat, turning occasionally, for 5–10 minutes, or until golden. Transfer to a plate with a slotted spoon.

Add the onion and red pepper to the casserole. Cook over a low heat, stirring occasionally, for 5 minutes, or until softened. Sprinkle in any remaining seasoned flour and cook, stirring constantly, for 1 minute. Gradually stir in the stock, then add the raisins, chopped tomatoes, chilli powder, cinnamon, cumin and chocolate. Season to taste with salt and pepper. Bring to the boil, stirring constantly.

Return the turkey to the casserole, cover and cook in the preheated oven for 50 minutes. Serve immediately, garnished with sprigs of coriander.

SERVES 4

55 g/2 oz plain flour

salt and pepper

4 turkey breast fillets

3 tbsp corn oil

1 onion, thinly sliced

1 red pepper, deseeded and sliced

300 ml/10 fl oz chicken stock

25 g/1 oz raisins

4 tomatoes, peeled, deseeded
   and chopped

1 tsp chilli powder

$^1/_2$ tsp ground cinnamon

pinch of ground cumin

25 g/1 oz plain chocolate, finely
   chopped or grated

sprigs of fresh coriander, to garnish

Italian Turkey Steaks

Preheat the grill to medium. Heat the oil in a flameproof casserole or heavy-based frying pan. Add the turkey escalopes and cook over a medium heat for 5–10 minutes, turning occasionally, until golden. Transfer to a plate.

Add the red pepper and onion to the frying pan and cook over a low heat, stirring occasionally, for 5 minutes, or until softened. Add the garlic and cook for a further 2 minutes.

Return the turkey to the frying pan and add the passata, wine and marjoram. Season to taste with salt and pepper. Bring to the boil, then reduce the heat, cover and simmer, stirring occasionally, for 25–30 minutes, or until the turkey is cooked through and tender.

Stir in the cannellini beans and simmer for a further 5 minutes. Sprinkle the breadcrumbs over the top and place under the preheated grill for 2–3 minutes, or until golden. Serve, garnished with fresh basil sprigs.

SERVES 4

1 tbsp olive oil

4 turkey escalopes or steaks

2 red peppers, deseeded and sliced

1 red onion, sliced

2 garlic cloves, finely chopped

300 ml/10 fl oz passata

150 ml/5 fl oz medium white wine

1 tbsp chopped fresh marjoram

salt and pepper

400 g/14 oz canned cannellini
  beans, drained and rinsed

3 tbsp fresh white breadcrumbs

fresh basil sprigs, to garnish

Duck Legs with Olives

Put the duck legs in the bottom of a flameproof casserole or a large, heavy-based frying pan with a tight-fitting lid. Add the tomatoes, garlic, onion, carrot, celery, thyme and olives and stir together. Season with salt and pepper to taste.

Turn the heat to high and cook, uncovered, until the ingredients begin to bubble. Reduce the heat to low, cover tightly and simmer for 1¼–1½ hours until the duck is very tender. Check occasionally and add a little water if the mixture appears to be drying out.

When the duck is tender, transfer it to a serving platter, cover and keep hot in a preheated warm oven. Leave the casserole uncovered, increase the heat to medium and cook, stirring, for about 10 minutes until the mixture forms a sauce. Stir in the orange rind, then taste and adjust the seasoning if necessary.

Mash the tender garlic cloves with a fork and spread over the duck legs. Spoon the sauce over the top. Serve at once.

SERVES 4

4 duck legs, all visible fat trimmed off

800 g/1 lb 12 oz canned tomatoes, chopped

8 garlic cloves, peeled, but left whole

1 large onion, chopped

1 carrot, finely chopped

1 celery stick, finely chopped

3 sprigs fresh thyme

100 g/3½ oz Spanish green olives in brine, stuffed with pimientos, garlic or almonds, drained and rinsed

salt and pepper

1 tsp finely grated orange rind

Duck Jambalaya-style Stew

Remove and discard the skin and any fat from the duck breasts. Cut the flesh into bite-sized pieces.

Heat half the oil in a large deep frying pan and cook the duck, gammon and chorizo over a high heat, stirring frequently, for 5 minutes, or until browned on all sides and sealed. Using a slotted spoon, remove from the frying pan and set aside.

Add the onion, garlic, celery and chillies to the frying pan and cook over a medium heat, stirring frequently, for 5 minutes, or until softened. Add the green pepper, then stir in the stock, oregano, tomatoes and hot pepper sauce.

Bring to the boil, then reduce the heat and return the duck, gammon and chorizo to the frying pan. Cover and simmer, stirring occasionally, for 20 minutes, or until the duck and gammon are tender.

Serve immediately, garnished with parsley and accompanied by a green salad and rice.

SERVES 4

4 duck breasts, about 150 g/5^1/$_2$ oz each

2 tbsp olive oil

225 g/8 oz piece gammon, cut into small chunks

225 g/8 oz chorizo, outer casing removed

1 onion, chopped

3 garlic cloves, chopped

3 celery sticks, chopped

1–2 fresh red chillies, deseeded and chopped

1 green pepper, deseeded and chopped

600 ml/1 pint chicken stock

1 tbsp chopped fresh oregano

400 g/14 oz canned chopped tomatoes

1–2 tsp hot pepper sauce, or to taste

chopped fresh flat-leaf parsley, to garnish

green salad, to serve

freshly cooked rice, to serve

Fish & Seafood Suppers

From fiery fish curries to rich Mediterranean seafood stews and from mussels to swordfish, these recipes prove once and for all that cooking – and eating – fish is not a chore but a pleasure. Even fussy children will be intrigued to open up tasty little fish parcels baked in the oven. Classic fish and seafood dishes are the perfect choice for easy and impressive entertaining, while roasted fish will prove to be a revelation even to confirmed meat-eaters.

Catalan Fish Stew

Put the saffron threads in a heatproof jug with the water and leave for at least 10 minutes to infuse.

Heat the oil in a large, heavy-based flameproof casserole over a medium–high heat. Reduce the heat to low and cook the onion, stirring occasionally, for 10 minutes, or until golden but not browned. Stir in the garlic, thyme, bay leaves and red peppers and cook, stirring frequently, for 5 minutes, or until the peppers are softened and the onions have softened further.

Add the tomatoes and paprika and simmer, stirring frequently, for a further 5 minutes.

Stir in the stock, the saffron and its soaking liquid and the almonds and bring to the boil, stirring. Reduce the heat and simmer for 5–10 minutes, until the sauce reduces and thickens. Season to taste with salt and pepper.

Meanwhile, clean the mussels and clams by scrubbing or scraping the shells and pulling out any beards that are attached to the mussels. Discard any with broken shells or any that refuse to close when tapped.

Gently stir the hake into the stew so that it doesn't break up, then add the prawns, mussels and clams. Reduce the heat to very low, cover and simmer for 5 minutes, or until the hake is opaque, the mussels and clams have opened and the prawns have turned pink. Discard any mussels or clams that remain closed. Serve immediately with plenty of thick crusty bread for soaking up the juices.

SERVES 4–6

large pinch of saffron threads

4 tbsp almost-boiling water

6 tbsp olive oil

1 large onion, chopped

2 garlic cloves, finely chopped

1¹/₂ tbsp chopped fresh thyme leaves

2 bay leaves

2 red peppers, deseeded and roughly chopped

800 g/1 lb 12 oz canned chopped tomatoes

1 tsp smoked paprika

250 ml/9 fl oz fish stock

140 g/5 oz blanched almonds, toasted and finely ground

salt and pepper

12–16 live mussels

12–16 live clams

600 g/1 lb 5 oz thick boned hake or cod fillets, skinned and cut into 5-cm/2-inch chunks

12–16 raw prawns, peeled and deveined

thick crusty bread, to serve

Squid with Parsley & Pine Kernels

Place the sultanas in a small bowl, cover with lukewarm water and set aside for 15 minutes to plump up.

Meanwhile, heat the olive oil in a heavy-based saucepan. Add the parsley and garlic and cook over a low heat, stirring frequently, for 3 minutes. Add the squid and cook, stirring occasionally, for 5 minutes.

Increase the heat to medium, pour in the wine and cook until it has almost completely evaporated. Stir in the passata and season to taste with chilli powder and salt. Lower the heat again, cover and simmer gently, stirring occasionally, for 45–50 minutes, until the squid is almost tender.

Drain the sultanas and stir them into the saucepan with the pine kernels. Let simmer for a further 10 minutes, then serve immediately garnished with the reserved chopped parsley.

SERVES 4

85 g/3 oz sultanas

5 tbsp olive oil

6 tbsp chopped fresh flat-leaf parsley, plus extra to garnish

2 garlic cloves, chopped finely

800 g/1 lb 12 oz prepared squid, sliced, or squid rings

125 ml/4 fl oz dry white wine

500 g/1 lb 2 oz passata

pinch of chilli powder

salt

85 g/3 oz pine kernels, chopped finely

Seafood in Saffron Sauce

Clean the mussels and clams by scrubbing or scraping the shells and pulling out any beards that are attached to the mussels. Discard any with broken shells or any that refuse to close when tapped.

Heat the oil in a large, flameproof casserole and cook the onion with the saffron, thyme and a pinch of salt over a low heat, stirring occasionally, for 5 minutes, or until softened. Add the garlic and cook, stirring, for 2 minutes.

Add the tomatoes, wine and stock, season to taste with salt and pepper and stir well. Bring to the boil, then reduce the heat and simmer for 15 minutes.

Add the fish chunks and simmer for a further 3 minutes. Add the clams, mussels and squid rings and simmer for a further 5 minutes, or until the mussels and clams have opened. Discard any that remain closed. Stir in the basil and serve immediately, accompanied by plenty of fresh bread to mop up the broth.

SERVES 4

225 g/8 oz live mussels

225 g/8 oz live clams

2 tbsp olive oil

1 onion, sliced

pinch of saffron threads

1 tbsp chopped fresh thyme

salt and pepper

2 garlic cloves, finely chopped

800 g/1 lb 12 oz canned tomatoes, drained and chopped

175 ml/6 fl oz dry white wine

2 litres/$3^1/_2$ pints fish stock

350 g/12 oz red mullet fillets, cut into bite-sized chunks

450 g/1 lb monkfish fillets, cut into bite-sized chunks

225 g/8 oz raw squid rings

2 tbsp fresh shredded basil leaves

fresh bread, to serve

Moroccan Fish Tagine

Heat the olive oil in a flameproof casserole. Add the onion and cook gently over a very low heat, stirring occasionally, for 10 minutes, or until softened, but not coloured. Add the saffron, cinnamon, ground coriander, cumin and turmeric and cook for a further 30 seconds, stirring constantly.

Add the tomatoes and fish stock and stir well. Bring to the boil, reduce the heat, cover and simmer for 15 minutes. Uncover and simmer for 20–35 minutes, or until thickened.

Cut each red mullet in half, then add the fish pieces to the casserole, pushing them down into the liquid. Simmer the stew for a further 5–6 minutes, or until the fish is just cooked.

Carefully stir in the olives, preserved lemon and chopped coriander. Season to taste with salt and pepper and serve immediately with couscous.

SERVES 4

2 tbsp olive oil

1 large onion, finely chopped

pinch of saffron threads

$^1/_2$ tsp ground cinnamon

1 tsp ground coriander

$^1/_2$ tsp ground cumin

$^1/_2$ tsp ground turmeric

200 g/7 oz canned chopped tomatoes

300 ml/10 fl oz fish stock

4 small red mullet, cleaned, boned and heads and tails removed

55 g/2 oz stoned green olives

1 tbsp chopped preserved lemon

3 tbsp chopped fresh coriander

salt and pepper

freshly cooked couscous, to serve

Seafood Chilli

Place the prawns, scallops, monkfish chunks and lime slices in a large, non-metallic dish with ¼ teaspoon of the chilli powder, ¼ teaspoon of the ground cumin, 1 tablespoon of the chopped coriander, half the garlic, the fresh chilli and 1 tablespoon of the oil. Cover with clingfilm and leave to marinate for up to 1 hour.

Meanwhile, heat 1 tablespoon of the remaining oil in a flameproof casserole or large, heavy-based saucepan. Add the onion, the remaining garlic and the red and yellow peppers and cook over a low heat, stirring occasionally, for 5 minutes, or until softened. Add the remaining chilli powder, the remaining cumin, the cloves, cinnamon and cayenne pepper with the remaining oil, if necessary, and season to taste with salt. Cook, stirring, for 5 minutes, then gradually stir in the stock and the tomatoes and their juices. Partially cover and simmer for 25 minutes.

Add the beans to the tomato mixture and spoon the fish and shellfish on top. Cover and cook for 10 minutes, or until the fish and shellfish are cooked through. Sprinkle with the remaining coriander and serve.

SERVES 4

115 g/4 oz raw prawns, peeled

250 g/9 oz prepared scallops, thawed if frozen

115 g/4 oz monkfish fillet, cut into chunks

1 lime, peeled and thinly sliced

1 tbsp chilli powder

1 tsp ground cumin

3 tbsp chopped fresh coriander

2 garlic cloves, finely chopped

1 fresh green chilli, deseeded and chopped

3 tbsp corn oil

1 onion, roughly chopped

1 red pepper, deseeded and roughly chopped

1 yellow pepper, deseeded and roughly chopped

¼ tsp ground cloves

pinch of ground cinnamon

pinch of cayenne pepper

salt

350 ml/12 fl oz fish stock

400 g/14 oz canned chopped tomatoes

400 g/14 oz canned red kidney beans, drained and rinsed

Mediterranean Fish Stew

Heat the oil in a large, flameproof casserole. Add the onion, saffron, thyme and a pinch of salt. Cook over a low heat, stirring occasionally, for 5 minutes, or until the onion has softened.

Add the garlic and cook for a further 2 minutes, then add the drained tomatoes and pour in the stock and wine. Season to taste with salt and pepper, bring the mixture to the boil, then reduce the heat and simmer for 15 minutes.

Add the chunks of mullet and monkfish and simmer for 3 minutes. Add the clams and squid and simmer for 5 minutes, or until the clam shells have opened. Discard any clams that remain closed. Tear in the basil and stir. Serve garnished with the extra basil leaves.

SERVES 4

2 tbsp olive oil

1 onion, sliced

pinch of saffron threads, lightly crushed

1 tbsp chopped fresh thyme

salt and pepper

2 garlic cloves, finely chopped

800 g/1 lb 12 oz canned chopped tomatoes, drained

2 litres/$3^1/_2$ pints fish stock

175 ml/6 fl oz dry white wine

350 g/12 oz red mullet fillets, cut into chunks

450 g/1 lb monkfish fillets, cut into chunks

450 g/1 lb fresh clams, scrubbed

225 g/8 oz squid rings

2 tbsp fresh basil leaves, plus extra to garnish

Moules Marinières

Clean the mussels by scrubbing or scraping the shells and pulling off any beards. Discard any with broken shells or any that refuse to close when tapped with a knife. Rinse the mussels under cold running water.

Pour the wine into a large, heavy-based saucepan, add the shallots and bouquet garni and season to taste with pepper. Bring to the boil over a medium heat. Add the mussels, cover tightly and cook, shaking the saucepan occasionally, for 5 minutes. Remove and discard the bouquet garni and any mussels that remain closed. Divide the mussels among 4 soup plates with a slotted spoon. Tilt the casserole to let any sand settle, then spoon the cooking liquid over the mussels, garnish with a bay leaf, and serve immediately with bread.

SERVES 4

2 kg/4 lb 8 oz live mussels

300 ml/10 fl oz dry white wine

6 shallots, finely chopped

1 bouquet garni

pepper

4 bay leaves, to garnish

crusty bread, to serve

Roasted Seafood

Preheat the oven to 200°C/400°F/Gas Mark 6.

Scrub the potatoes to remove any dirt. Cut any large potatoes in half. Parboil the potatoes in a saucepan of boiling water for 10–15 minutes. Place the potatoes in a large roasting tin together with the onions, courgettes, garlic, lemons and rosemary sprigs.

Pour over the oil and toss to coat all the vegetables in it. Roast in the oven for 30 minutes, turning occasionally, until the potatoes are tender.

Once the potatoes are tender, add the prawns, squid and tomatoes, tossing to coat them in the oil, and roast for 5 minutes. All the vegetables should be cooked through and slightly charred for full flavour. Transfer the roasted seafood and vegetables to warmed serving plates and serve hot.

SERVES 4

600 g/1 lb 5 oz new potatoes

3 red onions, cut into wedges

2 courgettes, cut into chunks

8 garlic cloves, peeled but left whole

2 lemons, cut into wedges

4 fresh rosemary sprigs

4 tbsp olive oil

350 g/12 oz unpeeled raw prawns

2 small raw squid, cut into rings

4 tomatoes, quartered

Goan-Style Seafood Curry

Heat the oil in a kadhai, wok or large frying pan over a high heat. Add the mustard seeds and stir them around for about 1 minute, or until they jump. Stir in the curry leaves.

Add the shallots and garlic and stir for about 5 minutes, or until the shallots are golden. Stir in the turmeric, coriander and chilli powder and continue stirring for about 30 seconds.

Add the dissolved creamed coconut. Bring to the boil, then reduce the heat to medium and stir for about 2 minutes.

Reduce the heat to low, add the fish and simmer for 1 minute, spooning the sauce over the fish and very gently stirring it around. Add the prawns and continue to simmer for 4–5 minutes longer until the fish flesh flakes easily and the prawns turn pink and curl.

Add half the lime juice, then taste and add more lime juice and salt to taste. Sprinkle with the lime rind and serve with lime wedges.

SERVES 4–6

3 tbsp vegetable or groundnut oil

1 tbsp black mustard seeds

12 fresh curry leaves or 1 tbsp dried

6 shallots, finely chopped

1 garlic clove, crushed

1 tsp ground turmeric

$^1/_2$ ground coriander

$^1/_4$–$^1/_2$ tsp chilli powder

140 g/5 oz creamed coconut, grated and dissolved in 300 ml/10 fl oz boiling water

500 g/1 lb 2 oz skinless, boneless white fish, such as monkfish or cod, cut into large chunks

450 g/1 lb large raw prawns, peeled and deveined

finely grated rind and juice of 1 lime

salt

lime wedges, to serve

Jambalaya

Heat the vegetable oil in a large frying pan over a low heat. Add the onions, pepper, celery and garlic and cook for 8–10 minutes until all the vegetables have softened. Add the paprika and cook for a further 30 seconds. Add the chicken and sausages and cook for 8–10 minutes until lightly browned. Add the tomatoes and cook for 2–3 minutes until they have collapsed.

Add the rice to the pan and stir well. Pour in the hot stock, oregano and bay leaves and stir well. Cover and simmer for 10 minutes.

Add the prawns and stir. Cover again and cook for a further 6–8 minutes until the rice is tender and the prawns are cooked through.

Stir in the spring onions and parsley and season to taste with salt and pepper. Transfer to a large serving dish, garnish with chopped fresh herbs and serve.

SERVES 4

2 tbsp vegetable oil

2 onions, chopped roughly

1 green pepper, deseeded and roughly chopped

2 celery sticks, chopped roughly

3 garlic cloves, chopped finely

2 tsp paprika

300 g/1^1/$_2$ oz skinless, boneless chicken breasts, chopped

100 g/3^1/$_2$ oz kabanos sausages, chopped

3 tomatoes, peeled and chopped

450 g/1 lb long-grain rice

850 ml/1^1/$_2$ pints hot chicken or fish stock

1 tsp dried oregano

2 bay leaves

12 large raw prawns

4 spring onions, chopped finely

2 tbsp chopped fresh parsley

salt and pepper

chopped fresh herbs, to garnish

Prawns with Coconut Rice

Place the mushrooms in a small bowl, cover with hot water and set aside to soak for 30 minutes. Drain, then cut off and discard the stalks and slice the caps.

Heat 1 tablespoon of the oil in a wok and stir-fry the spring onions, coconut and chilli for 2–3 minutes, until lightly browned. Add the mushrooms and stir-fry for 3–4 minutes.

Add the rice and stir-fry for 2–3 minutes, then add the stock and bring to the boil. Lower the heat and add the coconut milk. Simmer for 10–15 minutes, until the rice is tender. Stir in the prawns and basil, heat through and serve.

SERVES 4

115 g/4 oz dried Chinese mushrooms

2 tbsp vegetable or groundnut oil

6 spring onions, chopped

55 g/2 oz desiccated coconut

1 fresh green chilli, deseeded and chopped

225 g/8 oz jasmine rice

150 ml/$1/4$ pint fish stock

400 ml/14 fl oz coconut milk

350 g/12 oz cooked peeled prawns

6 sprigs fresh Thai basil

Prawn Biryani

Soak the saffron in the tepid water for 10 minutes. Put the shallots, garlic, spices and salt into a spice grinder or mortar and pestle and grind to a paste.

Heat the ghee in a saucepan and add the mustard seeds. When they start to pop, add the prawns and stir over a high heat for 1 minute. Stir in the spice mix, then the coconut milk and yogurt. Simmer for 20 minutes.

Spoon the prawn mixture into serving bowls. Top with the freshly cooked basmati rice and drizzle over the saffron water. Serve, garnished with the flaked almonds, spring onion and sprigs of coriander.

SERVES 8

1 tsp saffron strands

50 ml/2 fl oz tepid water

2 shallots, chopped coarsely

3 garlic cloves, crushed

1 tsp chopped fresh root ginger

2 tsp coriander seeds

$^1/_2$ tsp black peppercorns

2 cloves

seeds from 2 green cardamom pods

2.5-cm/1-inch piece cinnamon stick

1 tsp ground turmeric

1 fresh green chilli, chopped

$^1/_2$ tsp salt

2 tbsp ghee

1 tsp whole black mustard seeds

500 g/1 lb 2 oz uncooked tiger
  prawns in their shells, or
    400 g/14 oz uncooked and peeled

300 ml/$^1/_2$ pint coconut milk

300 ml/$^1/_2$ pint low-fat natural
  yogurt

freshly cooked basmati rice,
  to serve

to garnish

flaked almonds, toasted

1 spring onion, sliced

sprigs of fresh coriander

Prawn & Chicken Paella

Soak the mussels in lightly salted water for 10 minutes. Put the saffron threads and water in a small bowl or cup and let infuse for a few minutes. Meanwhile, put the rice in a sieve and rinse in cold water until the water runs clear. Set aside.

Clean the mussels by scrubbing the shells and pulling out any beards that are attached to them. Discard any with broken shells or any that refuse to close when tapped. Set aside.

Heat 3 tablespoons of the oil in a 30-cm/12-inch paella pan or ovenproof casserole. Cook the chicken thighs over medium–high heat, turning frequently, for 5 minutes, or until golden and crispy. Using a slotted spoon, transfer to a bowl. Add the chorizo to the pan and cook, stirring, for 1 minute, or until beginning to crisp. Add to the chicken.

Heat the remaining oil in the pan and cook the onions, stirring frequently, for 2 minutes, then add the garlic and paprika and cook for a further 3 minutes, or until the onions are soft but not browned.

Add the drained rice, beans and peas and stir until coated in oil. Return the chicken and chorizo and any accumulated juices to the pan. Stir in the stock, saffron and its soaking liquid, and salt and pepper to taste and bring to the boil, stirring constantly. Reduce the heat to low and let simmer, uncovered and without stirring, for 15 minutes, or until the rice is almost tender and most of the liquid has been absorbed.

Arrange the mussels, prawns and red peppers on top, then cover and simmer, without stirring, for a further 5 minutes, or until the prawns turn pink and the mussels open. Discard any mussels that remain closed. Taste and adjust the seasoning if necessary. Sprinkle with the parsley and serve immediately.

SERVES 6–8

16 live mussels

$^1/_2$ tsp saffron threads

2 tbsp hot water

350 g/12 oz cups medium-grain paella rice

6 tbsp olive oil

6–8 unboned, chicken thighs, skin-on but with excess fat removed

140 g/5 oz Spanish chorizo sausage, casing removed, cut into 5-mm/ $^1/_4$-inch slices

2 large onions, chopped

4 large garlic cloves, crushed

1 tsp mild or hot Spanish paprika, to taste

100 g/3$^1/_2$ oz green beans, chopped

125 g/4$^1/_2$ oz frozen peas

1.3 litres/2$^1/_4$ pints fish, chicken or vegetable stock

salt and pepper

16 raw prawns, peeled and deveined

2 red peppers, halved and deseeded, then grilled, peeled and sliced

35 g/1$^1/_4$ oz fresh chopped parsley, to garnish

Genoese Seafood Risotto

Heat the oil with 25 g/1 oz of the butter in a deep saucepan over a medium heat until the butter has melted. Add the garlic and cook, stirring, for 1 minute.

Reduce the heat, add the rice and mix to coat in oil and butter. Cook, stirring constantly, for 2–3 minutes, or until the grains are translucent.

Gradually add the hot stock, a ladle at a time. Stir constantly and add more liquid as the rice absorbs each addition. Increase the heat to medium so that the liquid bubbles. Cook for 20 minutes, or until all the liquid is absorbed and the rice is creamy.

About 5 minutes before the rice is ready, add the seafood and oregano to the saucepan and mix well.

Remove the saucepan from the heat and season to taste. Add the remaining butter and mix well, then stir in the grated cheese until it melts. Spoon onto warmed plates and serve immediately, garnished with extra oregano.

SERVES 4

1 tbsp olive oil

55 g/2 oz butter

2 garlic cloves, chopped

350 g/12 oz risotto rice

1.3 litres/2^1/$_4$ pints fish or chicken stock

250 g/9 oz mixed cooked seafood, such as prawns, squid, mussels and clams

2 tbsp chopped fresh oregano, plus extra to garnish

salt and pepper

55 g/2 oz freshly grated pecorino or Parmesan cheese

Sicilian Tuna

Whisk all the marinade ingredients together in a small bowl. Put the tuna steaks in a large, shallow dish and spoon over 4 tablespoons of the marinade, turning until well coated. Cover and leave to marinate in the refrigerator for 30 minutes. Reserve the remaining marinade.

Heat a ridged griddle pan over a high heat. Put the fennel and onions in a separate bowl, add the oil and toss well to coat. Add to the griddle pan and cook for 5 minutes on each side until just beginning to colour. Transfer to 4 warmed serving plates, drizzle with the reserved marinade and keep warm.

Add the tuna steaks to the griddle pan and cook, turning once, for 4–5 minutes until firm to the touch but still moist inside. Transfer the tuna to the serving plates and serve immediately with crusty rolls.

SERVES 4

for the marinade

125 ml/4 fl oz extra-virgin olive oil

4 garlic cloves, finely chopped

4 fresh red chillies, deseeded and finely chopped

juice and finely grated rind of 2 lemons

4 tbsp finely chopped fresh flat-leaf parsley

salt and pepper

4 tuna steaks, about 140 g/5 oz each

2 fennel bulbs, thickly sliced lengthways

2 red onions, sliced

2 tbsp extra-virgin olive oil

crusty rolls, to serve

Swordfish with Tomatoes & Olives

Heat the oil in a large, heavy-based frying pan. Add the onion and celery and cook over a low heat, stirring occasionally, for 5 minutes, or until softened.

Meanwhile, roughly chop half the olives. Stir the chopped and whole olives into the saucepan with the tomatoes and capers and season to taste with salt and pepper.

Bring to the boil, then reduce the heat, cover and simmer gently, stirring occasionally, for 15 minutes.

Add the swordfish steaks to the frying pan and return to the boil. Cover and simmer, turning the fish once, for 20 minutes, or until the fish is cooked and the flesh flakes easily. Transfer the fish to serving plates and spoon the sauce over them. Garnish with fresh parsley sprigs and serve immediately.

SERVES 4

2 tbsp olive oil

1 onion, finely chopped

1 celery stick, finely chopped

115 g/4 oz green olives, stoned

450 g/1 lb tomatoes, chopped

3 tbsp bottled capers, drained

salt and pepper

4 swordfish steaks, about
    140 g/5 oz each

fresh flat-leaf parsley sprigs,
    to garnish

Monkfish Parcels

Preheat the oven to 190°C/375°F/Gas Mark 5. Cut 4 large pieces of foil, each about 23 cm/9 inches square. Brush them lightly with a little of the oil, then divide the courgettes and pepper among them.

Rinse the fish fillets under cold running water and pat dry with kitchen paper. Cut them in half, then put 1 piece on top of each pile of courgettes and pepper. Cut the bacon rashers in half and lay 3 pieces across each piece of fish. Season to taste with salt and pepper, drizzle over the remaining oil and close up the parcels. Seal tightly, transfer to an ovenproof dish and bake in the preheated oven for 25 minutes.

Remove from the oven, open each foil parcel slightly and serve with pasta and slices of olive bread.

SERVES 4

4 tsp olive oil

2 courgettes, sliced

1 large red pepper, peeled, deseeded and cut into strips

2 monkfish fillets, about 125 g/ 4½ oz each, skin and membrane removed

6 smoked streaky bacon rashers

salt and pepper

freshly cooked pasta, to serve

slices of olive bread, to serve

Roasted Monkfish

Preheat the oven to 200°C/400°F/Gas Mark 6. Remove the central bone from the fish if not already removed and make small slits down each fillet. Cut 2 of the garlic cloves into thin slivers and insert into the fish. Place the fish on a sheet of greaseproof paper, season with salt and pepper to taste and drizzle over 1 tablespoon of the oil. Bring the top edges together. Form into a pleat and fold over, then fold the ends underneath, completely encasing the fish. Reserve.

Put the remaining garlic cloves and all the vegetables into a roasting tin and drizzle with the remaining oil, turning the vegetables so that they are well coated in the oil.

Roast in the preheated oven for 20 minutes, turning occasionally. Put the fish parcel on top of the vegetables and cook for a further 15–20 minutes, or until the vegetables are tender and the fish is cooked.

Remove from the oven and open up the parcel. Cut the monkfish into thick slices. Arrange the vegetables on warmed serving plates, top with the fish slices and sprinkle with the basil. Serve immediately.

SERVES 4

675 g/1 lb 8 oz monkfish tail, skinned

4–5 large garlic cloves, peeled

salt and pepper

3 tbsp olive oil

1 onion, cut into wedges

1 small aubergine, about 300 g/ 10½ oz, cut into chunks

1 red pepper, deseeded, cut into wedges

1 yellow pepper, deseeded, cut into wedges

1 large courgette, about 225 g/8 oz, cut into wedges

1 tbsp shredded fresh basil, to garnish

Vegetable Heaven

Eating plenty of healthy vegetables every day could not be easier or more fun than with this superb collection of international recipes. Whether your taste is for a medley of summer flavours, a spicy curry, a hearty winter warmer, a flavoursome gratin or an elegant risotto, these delicious and easy-to-prepare vegetable dishes are sure to fit the bill. Economical, irresistible, nourishing and all in a single pot – what more could anyone want?

Italian Vegetable Stew

Finely chop the garlic and dice the squash. Put them in a large, heavy-based saucepan with a tight-fitting lid. Add the onion, leeks, aubergine, celeriac, turnips, tomatoes, carrot, courgette, red peppers, fennel, chard, bay leaves, fennel seeds, chilli powder, thyme, oregano, sugar, oil, stock and half the basil. Mix together well, then bring to the boil.

Reduce the heat, cover and simmer for 30 minutes, or until all the vegetables are tender.

Sprinkle in the remaining basil and the parsley and season to taste with salt and pepper. Serve immediately, sprinkled with the cheese.

SERVES 4

4 garlic cloves

1 small acorn squash, deseeded and peeled

1 red onion, sliced

2 leeks, sliced

1 aubergine, sliced

1 small celeriac, diced

2 turnips, sliced

2 plum tomatoes, chopped

1 carrot, sliced

1 courgette, sliced

2 red peppers, deseeded and chopped

1 fennel bulb, sliced

175 g/6 oz chard, chopped

2 bay leaves

$^1/_2$ tsp fennel seeds

$^1/_2$ tsp chilli powder

pinch each of dried thyme, dried oregano and sugar

125 ml/4 fl oz extra-virgin olive oil

225 ml/8 fl oz vegetable stock

25 g/1 oz fresh basil leaves, torn

4 tbsp chopped fresh parsley

salt and pepper

2 tbsp freshly grated Parmesan cheese, to garnish

Spring Stew

Heat the oil in a large, heavy-based saucepan, with a tight-fitting lid. Add the onions, celery, carrots and potatoes and cook, stirring frequently, for 5 minutes, or until softened. Add the stock, drained beans, bouquet garni and soy sauce, then bring to the boil. Reduce the heat, cover and simmer for 12 minutes.

Add the baby sweetcorn and broad beans and season to taste with salt and pepper. Simmer for a further 3 minutes.

Meanwhile, discard the outer leaves and hard central core from the cabbage and shred the leaves. Add to the saucepan and simmer for a further 3–5 minutes, or until all the vegetables are tender.

Blend the cornflour with the water, stir into the saucepan and cook, stirring, for 4–6 minutes, or until the liquid has thickened. Serve with a bowl of cheese for stirring into the stew.

SERVES 4

2 tbsp olive oil

4–8 baby onions, halved

2 celery sticks, cut into
5-mm/^{1}/$_4$-inch slices

225 g/8 oz baby carrots, scrubbed,
and halved if large

300 g/10^1/$_2$ oz new potatoes,
scrubbed and halved, or
quartered if large

850 ml–1.2 litres/1^1/$_2$–2 pints
vegetable stock

400 g/14 oz canned haricot beans,
drained and rinsed

1 fresh bouquet garni

1^1/$_2$–2 tbsp light soy sauce

85 g/3 oz baby sweetcorn

115 g/4 oz frozen or shelled fresh
broad beans, thawed if frozen

salt and pepper

^{1}/$_2$–1 Savoy or spring cabbage,
about 225 g/8 oz

1^1/$_2$ tbsp cornflour

2 tbsp cold water

55–85 g/2–3 oz Parmesan or
mature Cheddar cheese, grated,
to serve

Tuscan Bean Stew

Trim the fennel and reserve any feathery fronds, then cut the bulb into small strips. Heat the oil in a large, heavy-based saucepan with a tight-fitting lid, and cook the onion, garlic, chilli and fennel strips, stirring frequently, for 5–8 minutes, or until softened.

Add the aubergine and cook, stirring frequently, for 5 minutes. Blend the tomato purée with a little of the stock in a jug and pour over the fennel mixture, then add the remaining stock, and the tomatoes, vinegar and oregano. Bring to the boil, then reduce the heat, cover and simmer for 15 minutes, or until the tomatoes have begun to collapse.

Drain and rinse the beans, the drain again. Add them to the pan with the yellow pepper, courgette and olives. Simmer for a further 15 minutes, or until all the vegetables are tender. Taste and adjust the seasoning. Scatter with the Parmesan cheese shavings and serve garnished with the reserved fennel fronds, accompanied by polenta wedges or crusty bread.

SERVES 4

1 large fennel bulb

2 tbsp olive oil

1 red onion, cut into small wedges

2–4 garlic cloves, sliced

1 fresh green chilli, deseeded and
chopped

1 small aubergine, about 225 g/
8 oz, cut into chunks

2 tbsp tomato purée

450–600 ml/16 fl oz–1 pint
vegetable stock

450 g/1 lb ripe tomatoes

1 tbsp balsamic vinegar

a few sprigs fresh oregano

400 g/14 oz canned borlotti beans

400 g/14 oz canned flageolet beans

1 yellow pepper, deseeded and cut
into small strips

1 courgette, sliced into half moons

55 g/2 oz stoned black olives

salt and pepper

25 g/1 oz Parmesan cheese, freshly
shaved

polenta wedges or crusty bread,
to serve

Potato & Lemon Casserole

Heat the olive oil in a flameproof casserole. Add the onions and sauté over a medium heat, stirring frequently, for 3 minutes.

Add the garlic and cook for 30 seconds. Stir in the ground cumin, ground coriander and cayenne and cook, stirring constantly, for 1 minute.

Add the carrot, turnips, courgette and potatoes and stir to coat in the oil.

Add the lemon juice and rind and the vegetable stock. Season to taste with salt and pepper. Cover and cook over a medium heat, stirring occasionally, for 20–30 minutes until tender.

Remove the lid, sprinkle in the chopped fresh coriander and stir well. Serve immediately.

SERVES 4

100 ml/3^1/$_2$ fl oz olive oil

2 red onions, cut into 8 wedges

3 garlic cloves, crushed

2 tsp ground cumin

2 tsp ground coriander

pinch of cayenne pepper

1 carrot, thickly sliced

2 small turnips, quartered

1 courgette, sliced

500 g/1 lb 2 oz potatoes, thickly sliced

juice and grated rind of 2 large lemons

300 ml/10 fl oz vegetable stock

salt and pepper

2 tbsp chopped fresh coriander

Lentil & Rice Casserole

Place the lentils, rice and vegetable stock in a large flameproof casserole and cook over a low heat, stirring occasionally, for 20 minutes.

Add the leek, garlic, tomatoes and their can juice, ground cumin, chilli powder, garam masala, sliced pepper, broccoli, baby sweetcorn and French beans to the pan.

Bring the mixture to the boil, reduce the heat, cover and simmer for a further 10–15 minutes or until the vegetables are tender.

Add the shredded basil and season with salt and pepper to taste.

Garnish with fresh basil sprigs and serve immediately.

SERVES 4

225 g/8 oz red lentils

55 g/2 oz long-grain rice

1.2 litres/2 pints vegetable stock

1 leek, cut into chunks

3 garlic cloves, crushed

400 g/14 oz canned chopped tomatoes

1 tsp ground cumin

1 tsp chilli powder

1 tsp garam masala

1 red pepper, deseeded and sliced

100 g/3½ oz small broccoli florets

8 baby sweetcorn, halved lengthways

55 g/2 oz French beans, halved

1 tbsp shredded fresh basil

salt and pepper

fresh basil sprigs, to garnish

Vegetable Goulash

Put the sun-dried tomatoes in a small heatproof bowl, cover with almost boiling water and leave to soak for 15–20 minutes. Drain, reserving the soaking liquid.

Heat the oil in a large, heavy-based saucepan, with a tight-fitting lid, and cook the chillies, garlic and vegetables, stirring frequently, for 5–8 minutes until softened. Blend the tomato purée with a little of the stock in a jug and pour over the vegetable mixture, then add the remaining stock, lentils, the sun-dried tomatoes and their soaking liquid, and the paprika and thyme.

Bring to the boil, then reduce the heat, cover and simmer for 15 minutes. Add the fresh tomatoes and simmer for a further 15 minutes, or until the vegetables and lentils are tender. Serve topped with spoonfuls of soured cream, accompanied by crusty bread.

SERVES 4

15 g/^{1}/$_2$ oz sun-dried tomatoes, chopped

2 tbsp olive oil

^{1}/$_2$–1 tsp crushed dried chillies

2–3 garlic cloves, chopped

1 large onion, cut into small wedges

1 small celeriac, cut into small chunks

225 g/8 oz carrots, sliced

225 g/8 oz new potatoes, scrubbed and cut into chunks

1 small acorn squash, deseeded, peeled and cut into small chunks, about 225 g/8 oz prepared weight

2 tbsp tomato purée

300 ml/10 fl oz vegetable stock

450 g/1 lb canned Puy or green lentils, drained and rinsed

1–2 tsp hot paprika

a few sprigs fresh thyme

450 g/1 lb ripe tomatoes

soured cream, to garnish

crusty bread, to serve

Moroccan Hot Pot

Heat the oil in a large, heavy-based saucepan with a tight-fitting lid and cook the onion, garlic, chilli and aubergine, stirring frequently, for 5–8 minutes until softened.

Add the ginger, cumin, coriander and saffron and cook, stirring constantly, for 2 minutes. Bruise the cinnamon stick.

Add the cinnamon, squash, sweet potatoes, prunes, stock and tomatoes to the saucepan and bring to the boil. Reduce the heat, cover and simmer, stirring occasionally, for 20 minutes. Add the chickpeas to the saucepan and cook for a further 10 minutes. Discard the cinnamon and serve garnished with the fresh coriander.

SERVES 4

2 tbsp olive oil

1 Spanish onion, finely chopped

2–4 garlic cloves, crushed

1 fresh red chilli, deseeded and sliced

1 aubergine, about 225 g/8 oz, cut into small chunks

small piece fresh root ginger, peeled and grated

1 tsp ground cumin

1 tsp ground coriander

pinch of saffron threads or $1/2$ tsp turmeric

1–2 cinnamon sticks

$1/2$–1 butternut squash, about 450 g/1 lb, peeled, deseeded and cut into small chunks

225 g/8 oz sweet potatoes, cut into small chunks

85 g/3 oz ready-to-eat prunes

450–600 ml/16 fl oz–1 pint vegetable stock

4 tomatoes, chopped

400 g/14 oz canned chickpeas, drained and rinsed

1 tbsp chopped fresh coriander, to garnish

Chilli Bean Stew

Heat the oil in a large, heavy-based saucepan with a tight-fitting lid and cook the onion, garlic and chillies, stirring frequently, for 5 minutes, or until softened. Add the kidney and cannellini beans and the chickpeas. Blend the tomato purée with a little of the stock in a jug and pour over the bean mixture, then add the remaining stock. Bring to the boil, then reduce the heat and simmer for 10–15 minutes.

Add the red pepper, tomatoes, broad beans, and pepper to taste and simmer for a further 15–20 minutes, or until all the vegetables are tender. Stir in the chopped coriander.

Serve the stew topped with spoonfuls of soured cream and garnished with chopped coriander and a pinch of paprika.

SERVES 4–6

2 tbsp olive oil

1 onion, chopped

2–4 garlic cloves, chopped

2 fresh red chillies, deseeded and sliced

225 g/8 oz canned kidney beans, drained and rinsed

225 g/8 oz canned cannelini beans, drained and rinsed

225 g/8 oz canned chickpeas, drained and rinsed

1 tbsp tomato purée

700–850 ml/1^{1}/$_{4}$–1^{1}/$_{2}$ pints vegetable stock

1 red pepper, deseeded and chopped

4 tomatoes, roughly chopped

175 g/6 oz frozen or shelled fresh broad beans, thawed if frozen

pepper

1 tbsp chopped fresh coriander

soured cream, to serve

chopped fresh coriander, to garnish

paprika, to garnish

Roast Summer Vegetables

Preheat the oven to 200°C/400°F/Gas Mark 6. Cut the fennel, onions and tomatoes into wedges. Thickly slice the aubergine and courgettes. Cut the peppers into chunks. Brush a large ovenproof dish with a little of the oil. Arrange the prepared vegetables in the dish and tuck the garlic cloves and rosemary sprigs among them. Drizzle with the remaining oil and season to taste with plenty of freshly ground black pepper.

Roast the vegetables in the preheated oven for 20–25 minutes, turning once until they are tender and beginning to turn golden brown.

Serve the vegetables straight from the dish or transfer to a warmed serving platter. Serve immediately, with crusty bread, if you like, to mop up the juices.

SERVES 4

1 fennel bulb

2 red onions

2 beef tomatoes

1 aubergine

2 courgettes

1 yellow pepper, deseeded

1 red pepper, deseeded

1 orange pepper, deseeded

2 tbsp olive oil

4 garlic cloves

4 fresh rosemary sprigs

pepper

crusty bread, to serve (optional)

Ratatouille

Roughly chop the aubergines and courgettes, and deseed and chop the peppers. Slice the onions and finely chop the garlic.

Heat the oil in a large saucepan. Add the onions and cook over a low heat, stirring occasionally, for 5 minutes, or until softened. Add the garlic and cook, stirring frequently for a further 2 minutes.

Add the aubergines, courgettes and peppers. Increase the heat to medium and cook, stirring occasionally, until the peppers begin to colour. Add the bouquet garni, reduce the heat, cover and simmer gently for 40 minutes.

Stir in the chopped tomatoes and season to taste with salt and pepper. Re-cover the saucepan and simmer gently for a further 10 minutes. Remove and discard the bouquet garni. Serve warm or cold.

SERVES 4

2 aubergines

4 courgettes

2 yellow peppers

2 red peppers

2 onions

2 garlic cloves

150 ml/5 fl oz olive oil

1 bouquet garni

3 large tomatoes, peeled, deseeded
and roughly chopped

salt and pepper

Aubergine Gratin

Heat the oil in a flameproof casserole over a medium heat. Add the onion and cook for 5 minutes, or until soft. Add the garlic and cook for a few seconds, or until just beginning to colour. Using a perforated spoon, transfer the onion mixture to a plate.

Cook the aubergine slices in batches in the same flameproof casserole until they are just lightly browned. Transfer to another plate.

Preheat the oven to 200°C/400°F/Gas Mark 6. Arrange a layer of aubergine slices in the base of the casserole dish or a shallow ovenproof dish. Sprinkle with some of the parsley, thyme, salt and pepper. Add layers of onion, tomatoes and mozzarella, sprinkling parsley, thyme, salt and pepper over each layer.

Continue layering, finishing with a layer of aubergine slices. Sprinkle with the Parmesan. Bake, uncovered, in the preheated oven for 20–30 minutes, or until the top is golden and the aubergines are tender. Serve hot.

SERVES 2

4 tbsp olive oil

2 onions, chopped finely

2 garlic cloves, chopped very finely

2 aubergines, sliced thickly

3 tbsp chopped fresh flat-leaf parsley

$^1/_2$ tsp dried thyme

salt and pepper

400 g/14 oz canned chopped tomatoes

175 g/6 oz mozzarella, coarsely grated

6 tbsp freshly grated Parmesan

Vegetable Curry

Cut the aubergine, turnips and potatoes into 1-cm/$^1/_2$-inch cubes. Divide the cauliflower into small florets. Leave the button mushrooms whole or slice them thickly, if preferred. Slice the onion and carrots.

Heat the ghee in a large, heavy-based saucepan. Add the onion, turnips, potatoes and cauliflower and cook over a low heat, stirring frequently, for 3 minutes. Add the garlic, ginger, chillies, paprika, ground coriander and curry powder and cook, stirring, for 1 minute.

Add the stock, tomatoes, aubergine and mushrooms, and season to taste with salt. Cover and simmer, stirring occasionally, for 30 minutes, or until tender. Add the green pepper and carrots, cover and cook for a further 5 minutes.

Place the cornflour and coconut milk in a bowl, mix into a smooth paste and stir into the vegetable mixture. Add the ground almonds and simmer, stirring constantly, for 2 minutes. Taste and adjust the seasoning, if necessary. Transfer to warmed serving plates, garnish with coriander sprigs and serve immediately with freshly cooked rice.

SERVES 4

1 aubergine

225 g/8 oz turnips

350 g/12 oz new potatoes

225 g/8 oz cauliflower

225 g/8 oz button mushrooms

1 large onion

3 carrots

6 tbsp ghee

2 garlic cloves, crushed

4 tsp finely chopped fresh root ginger

1–2 fresh green chillies, deseeded and chopped

1 tbsp paprika

2 tsp ground coriander

1 tbsp mild or medium curry powder

450 ml/16 fl oz vegetable stock

400 g/14 oz canned chopped tomatoes

salt

1 green pepper, deseeded and sliced

1 tbsp cornflour

150 ml/5 fl oz coconut milk

2–3 tbsp ground almonds

fresh coriander sprigs, to garnish

freshly cooked rice, to serve

Cauliflower & Sweet Potato Curry

Heat the ghee in a large, heavy-based frying pan. Add the onions and Panch Phoran and cook over a low heat, stirring frequently, for 10 minutes, or until the onions are golden. Add the cauliflower, sweet potatoes and chillies and cook, stirring frequently, for 3 minutes.

Stir in the ginger paste, paprika, cumin, turmeric and chilli powder and cook, stirring constantly, for 3 minutes. Add the tomatoes and peas and stir in the yogurt and stock. Season with salt to taste, cover and simmer for 20 minutes, or until the vegetables are tender.

Sprinkle the garam masala over the curry, transfer to a warmed serving dish and serve immediately, garnished with fresh coriander sprigs.

SERVES 4

4 tbsp ghee or vegetable oil

2 onions, finely chopped

1 tsp Panch Phoran

1 cauliflower, broken into small florets

350 g/12 oz sweet potatoes, diced

2 fresh green chillies, deseeded and finely chopped

1 tsp ginger paste

2 tsp paprika

$1^1/_2$ tsp ground cumin

1 tsp ground turmeric

$^1/_2$ tsp chilli powder

3 tomatoes, quartered

225 g/8 oz fresh or frozen peas

3 tbsp natural yogurt

225 ml/8 fl oz vegetable stock or water

salt

1 tsp garam masala

fresh coriander sprigs, to garnish

Potato & Mushroom Bake

Preheat the oven to 190°C/375°F/Gas Mark 5. Grease a shallow, round ovenproof dish with the butter.

Layer a quarter of the potatoes in the base of the dish. Arrange one-third of the mushrooms on top of the potatoes and sprinkle with one-third of the rosemary, chives and garlic. Continue making the layers in the same order, and finish with a layer of potatoes on top.

Pour the double cream evenly over the top of the potatoes. Season to taste with salt and pepper.

Place the dish in the preheated oven, and cook for about 45 minutes, or until the bake is golden brown and piping hot.

Garnish with snipped chives and serve at once straight from the dish.

SERVES 4

2 tbsp butter

500 g/1 lb 2 oz waxy potatoes, thinly sliced and parboiled

150 g/5^1/$_2$ oz sliced mixed mushrooms

1 tbsp chopped fresh rosemary, plus extra to garnish

4 tbsp snipped chives, plus extra to garnish

2 garlic cloves, crushed

150 ml/5 fl oz double cream

salt and pepper

Parmesan Cheese Risotto with Mushrooms

Heat the oil in a deep saucepan. Add the rice and cook over a low heat, stirring constantly, for 2–3 minutes, until the grains are thoroughly coated in oil and translucent.

Add the garlic, onion, celery and pepper and cook, stirring frequently, for 5 minutes. Add the mushrooms and cook for 3–4 minutes. Stir in the oregano.

Gradually add the hot stock, a ladle at a time. Stir constantly and add more liquid as the rice absorbs each addition. Increase the heat to medium so that the liquid bubbles. Cook for 20 minutes, or until all the liquid is absorbed and the rice is creamy. Add the sun-dried tomatoes, if using, 5 minutes before the end of the cooking time and season to taste with salt and pepper.

Remove the risotto from the heat and stir in half the Parmesan until it melts. Transfer the risotto to warmed bowls. Top with the remaining cheese, garnish with flat-leaf parsley or bay leaves and serve immediately.

SERVES 6

2 tbsp olive oil or vegetable oil

225 g/8 oz risotto rice

2 garlic cloves, crushed

1 onion, chopped

2 celery sticks, chopped

1 red or green pepper, deseeded and chopped

225 g/8 oz mushrooms, thinly sliced

1 tbsp chopped fresh oregano or 1 tsp dried oregano

1 litre/1^{3}/$_{4}$ pints vegetable stock

55 g /2 oz sun-dried tomatoes in olive oil, drained and chopped (optional)

salt and pepper

55 g/2 oz finely grated Parmesan cheese

fresh flat-leaf parsley sprigs or bay leaves, to garnish

Risotto with Artichoke Hearts

Drain the artichoke hearts, reserving the liquid, and cut them into quarters.

Heat the oil with 25 g/1 oz of the butter in a deep saucepan over a medium heat until the butter has melted. Stir in the onion and cook gently, stirring occasionally, for 5 minutes, or until soft and starting to turn golden. Do not brown.

Add the rice and mix to coat in oil and butter. Cook, stirring constantly, for 2–3 minutes, or until the grains are translucent.

Gradually add the artichoke liquid and the hot stock, a ladle at a time. Stir constantly and add more liquid as the rice absorbs each addition. Increase the heat to medium so that the liquid bubbles. Cook for 15 minutes, then add the artichoke hearts. Cook for a further 5 minutes, or until all the liquid is absorbed and the rice is creamy. Season to taste with salt and pepper.

Remove the risotto from the heat and add the remaining butter. Mix well, then stir in the cheese until it melts. Season, if necessary. Spoon the risotto into warmed bowls, garnish with parsley sprigs and serve immediately.

SERVES 4

225 g/8 oz canned artichoke hearts
1 tbsp olive oil
40 g/1$^{1}/_{2}$ oz butter
1 small onion, finely chopped
280 g/10 oz risotto rice
1.2 litres/2 pints vegetable stock
salt and pepper
85 g/3 oz freshly grated Parmesan
   or Grana Padano cheese
fresh flat-leaf parsley sprigs,
   to garnish

Vegetarian Paella

Put the saffron threads and water in a small bowl or cup and let infuse for a few minutes.

Meanwhile, heat the oil in a paella pan or wide, shallow frying pan and cook the onion over medium heat, stirring, for 2–3 minutes, or until softened. Add the garlic, peppers and aubergine and cook, stirring frequently, for 5 minutes.

Add the rice and cook, stirring constantly, for 1 minute, or until glossy and coated. Pour in the stock and add the tomatoes, saffron and its soaking water and salt and pepper to taste. Bring to the boil, then reduce the heat and let simmer, shaking the frying pan frequently and stirring occasionally, for 15 minutes.

Stir in the mushrooms, green beans and pinto beans with their can juices. Cook for a further 10 minutes, then serve immediately.

SERVES 4–6

½ tsp saffron threads

2 tbsp hot water

6 tbsp olive oil

1 Spanish onion, sliced

3 garlic cloves, minced

1 red pepper, deseeded and sliced

1 orange pepper, deseeded and sliced

1 large aubergine, cubed

200 g/7 oz medium-grain paella rice

600 ml/1 pint vegetable stock

450 g/1 lb tomatoes, peeled and chopped

salt and pepper

115 g/4 oz button mushrooms, sliced

115 g/4 oz green beans, halved

400 g/14 oz canned pinto beans

Egg-Fried Rice with Vegetables

Heat the oil in a wok or large frying pan and fry the garlic and chillies for 2–3 minutes.

Add the mushrooms, mangetout and baby sweetcorn and stir-fry for 2–3 minutes before adding the soy sauce, sugar and basil. Stir in the rice.

Push the mixture to one side of the wok and add the eggs to the base and stir until lightly set before combining into the rice mixture.

If you wish to make the optional crispy onion topping, heat the oil in another frying pan and sauté the onions until crispy and brown. Serve the rice topped with the onions.

SERVES 4

2 tbsp vegetable or groundnut oil

2 garlic cloves, chopped finely

2 fresh red chillies, deseeded and chopped

115 g/4 oz mushrooms, sliced

50 g/2 oz mangetout, halved

50 g/2 oz baby sweetcorn, halved

3 tbsp Thai soy sauce

1 tbsp palm sugar or soft, light brown sugar

a few Thai basil leaves

350 g/12 oz rice, cooked and cooled

2 eggs, beaten

for the crispy onion topping (optional)

2 tbsp vegetable or groundnut oil

2 onions, sliced

Spiced Basmati Pilau

Place the rice in a sieve and wash well under cold running water. Drain. Trim off most of the broccoli stalk and cut the head into small florets, then quarter the stalk lengthways and cut diagonally into 1 cm/½ inch pieces.

Heat the oil in a large saucepan. Add the onions and broccoli stalks and cook over a low heat, stirring frequently, for 3 minutes. Add the mushrooms, rice, garlic and spices and cook for 1 minute, stirring, until the rice is coated in oil.

Add the stock and season to taste with salt and pepper. Stir in the broccoli florets and return the mixture to the boil. Cover, reduce the heat and cook over a low heat for 15 minutes without uncovering the pan.

Remove the pan from the heat and leave the pilau to stand for 5 minutes without uncovering. Remove the whole spices, add the raisins and pistachios and gently fork through to fluff up the grains. Serve the pilau hot.

SERVES 4

500 g/1 lb 2 oz basmati rice

175 g/6 oz broccoli, trimmed

6 tbsp vegetable oil

2 large onions, chopped

225 g/8 oz mushrooms, sliced

2 garlic cloves, crushed

6 cardamom pods, split

6 whole cloves

8 black peppercorns

1 cinnamon stick or piece of
    cassia bark

1 tsp turmeric

1.2 litres/2 pints vegetable stock
    or water

salt and pepper

60 g/2 oz seedless raisins

60 g/2 oz unsalted pistachios,
    roughly chopped